DR. YZABEL GANCE

AMBROSIA:
DIVINE PANACEA

A Roadmap to Happiness through God's Secret Gift

As seen in *The New York Times Book Review*

Heaven's grace, borne by a heavenly messenger, maps each soul's destined course; a sacred summons awaits our acceptance

AMBROSIA
Copyright © 2025 by Dr. Yzabel Gance

ISBN: 979-8894792057 (sc)
ISBN: 979-8894792064 (e)

The Reading Glass Books
1-888-420-3050
www.readingglassbooks.com
fulfillment@readingglassbooks.com

Dedication

This book celebrates the extraordinary gift of God's grace, a heavenly messenger divinely appointed, revealing a sacred reserve—a revelation for humanity—entrusted to me.

Acknowledgements

I am immensely indebted to numerous people whose insightful guidance and wisdom revealed life's breathtaking majesty. Their indispensable support was crucial in shaping my sense of well-being and happiness. First and foremost, I am deeply indebted to Dr. Jacob Pandian. His exceptional guidance and profoundly impactful mentorship have been transformative, a testament to his integrity and towering scholarly stature have impacting my life. Equally my deepest appreciation to all of my folks for their love and relentless support throughout their lives.

My heart overflows with immeasurable gratitude for Nob, my eternal guiding star figure, beacon illuminates my life's path. Her unparalleled righteousness, exceeding love and support, ceaseless spiritual and emotional sustenance have been a divine gift throughout my life. This acknowledgment, Nob, comes from the very core of my being.

My deepest gratitude goes out to each individual whose significant contributions were instrumental in bringing *AMBROSIA: Divine Panacea—A Roadmap to Happiness through God's Secret Gift* into existence. Your invaluable assistance was a profoundly enriching and cherished gift; particularly I owe significant to Ms. Lora Monroe, an executive project management.

I am profoundly indebted to Laurence, whose artistic brilliance has been a revelation. His imaginative flair, painstaking artistry, and singular creative perspective unveiled a universe of potential I never knew existed. His mentorship and unwavering support were crucial to my inner blossoming and metamorphosis. This remarkable journey of self-discovery would have remained uncharted without his exceptional contribution.

Contents

AMBROSIA: DIVINE PANACEA
A Roadmap to Happiness through God's Secret Gift

Dedication iii
Acknowledgements iv
Preface: The Secret of the Universe xi

PART - I: God's Intervention: Secret Gift—
Divine Hymns Prayer 1

    Who Was the Godsend, Cloaked in
       Human Form? 14
    Godsend' Essence and Role 17
    The Complex bond with Louis XV 23
    Godsend' Handwritten Manuscripts 25
    God's Providence 29

PART II: God's Decree and Promise 37

    God's Law of Destiny 38
    Secret Path to Victory 58
    Masterful Existence: Fair Play Wins! 65
    Fulfill Your Destiny 70
    The Law of Like Attracts Like 74

Break the Cycle of Misery............................77
The Holy Ark: Divine Revelation..............83
Hopes and Dreams......................................87
Live a Miraculous Life 93
Prayer: Conversation with God.................95
Faith: Secret of Manifestation 101
Urgent Plea: Unleash God's Gift 110

**PART III: God's Intervention: Miraculous
Manifestation**..115

GOLDEN BOUGH: Concealed Divine
    Wisdom...116
Invoking God's Presence............................121
Masterful Implementation-Successful
    Execution:...126
Forgiveness..128
Predestiny: God's Eternal Design 132
Abundant Blessings...................................139
Happiness..143
Love: Divine Decree 147
Prosperity...149
Power And Victory 155
Charisma 161
Youth, Beauty, Eternal Life.......................163
Light: A Source of Rejuvenation..............169
Healing...175
Chain of Ancestral Misery 177
Destroy Satanic Roots 183
Uproot Deadly Growth..............................190

Freedom from Malignant Triad: Fear,
    Doubt and Jealousy — A Soul Corroding
    Substance..194
End of Misery 196

Cited...199
Reference 204

Preface

The Secret of the Universe

An overwhelming impulse forces me to divulge the inexpressible. This reality surpasses the limitations of sensory perception; it exists outside the realm of the tangible. Its essence defies auditory comprehension, remaining silent beyond the reach of sound; it cannot be confined, grasped, or possessed; it is utterly ethereal. I am driven by an inner necessity to deliver the elusive truth of this encounter, a phenomenon that transcends the boundaries of our ordinary physical world. These pages hold a revelation, a sacred testament bestowed by God Almighty, delivering wisdom so profound it transcends human comprehension, a gift that resonates with unparalleled wisdom.

Ancient Greek thinkers, delving into existence's inscrutable abyss, grappled with the paradoxical nature of formless form and sightless sight – the limitless realm of the unimaginable. Humanity's cosmic understanding, throughout the ages, has been molded by a comprehensive, unifying worldview. The intricate interplay of inner perception and external manifestation generates a resonant feeling of interconnectedness, unveiling the universe's inherent essence through a radiant, evolutionary divine unfolding. Humanity's cosmic understanding across the ages has been molded by a unified vision—an indivisible marriage of internal intuition and empirical scrutiny. This reveals the universe's inherent essence as a radiant outpouring, a manifestation of its deepest self.

Timeless teachings reveal a deep and fundamental parity: Just as God, encompassing all existence—from celestial spheres to the mortal plane—holds infinite creation within its being, so too does the human consciousness cradle a boundless cosmos of its own. An expanse of desires, urges, anxieties, perceptions and a ceaseless flux of thoughts, both coherent and chaotic which it ceaselessly nurtures and sustains. A celestial wisdom, deeply ingrained in our DNA is a sacred gift, a legacy of cosmic understanding bestowed upon us. While theological interpretations vary, a core belief asserts a correspondence between the cosmic, overarching Creator—God in His immensity—and the indwelling Holy Spirit within humanity. Within dwells a divine spark, a miniature yet equally glorious reflection of God; a sanctified paragon mirroring the grandeur of the divine itself:

"Just as the universe contains the 10,000 things: creatures, world, stars, so our mind contains 10,000 things, namely desires, impulses, fears, sensations, thoughts logically connected or not it serves them."[1] *(Ancient wisdom proclaims. The cosmos, a boundless expanse, encompasses a myriad life forms, celestial bodies and the very fabric of reality itself, so our consciousness teems with a tumultuous myriad elements: yearnings, compulsions, anxieties, perceptions and cognition, each vying for dominance within the theater of the mind, regardless of internal coherence, it fulfills their purpose).*

Our inherent understanding of the universe, an inheritance encoded within our genetic blueprint, reveals God's endowment of unparalleled wisdom. While theological interpretations vary, a core principle posits a correspondence between the cosmic, overarching Creator—God in His immensity—and the indwelling Holy Spirit

---

1. Antient Doctrine-Unanimous

within humanity. This inner presence constitutes a smaller, yet equally magnificent, manifestation of the Divine, a sacred microcosm mirroring the majestic macrocosm.

Scripture reveals the astonishing, boundless potential of the human mind, a capacity that even God acknowledges the power of their collective effort and their potential to accomplish great things. *"And the Lord said, 'If as one people speaking the same language, they have begun to do this, then nothing they plan to do will be impossible for them.'"*, [2] *(God declared, "Their unified voice and shared tongue signal an unstoppable force; no ambition will remain beyond their collective reach).*

---

2.   Genesis 11:6

Part - I

God's Intervention: Secret Gift— Divine Hymns Prayer

As the Rays of the Sun Lighten
And Glide the Blackest Cloud,
So the Soul by Entering the Body
Of the God of Universe gives it Life
And Immortality; the Abject it Lifts Up.[1]

(God's radiant light, piercing darkness, bestows
life and immortality, elevating the lowly and
transmuting the crude into sublime glory).

---

1. Plotinus

1

Do you not know?

> *Have you not heard?*
> *Has it not been told you from the beginning?*
> *Have you not understood since the earth was founded?*
> *He sits enthroned above the circle of the earth,*
> *And its people are like grasshoppers.*
> *He stretches out the heavens like a canopy,*
> *And spreads them out like a tent to live in....*
> *Do you not know?*
> *Have you not heard?*
> **The lord is the everlasting god,**
> **The Creator of the ends of the earth.**
> *He will not grow tired or weary,*
> **And his understanding no one can fathom.**[2]

(Are you blind to this fundamental truth, unveiled from creation's dawn? Do you not grasp the cosmic implications of its origin?

He reigns supreme, his boundless power encompassing Earth. Their insignificant

---

2.   *Isaiah 40:21-22; 28*

numbers are lost in his vast creation; a mere ripple in an immeasurable ocean.

God's boundless expanse, a majestic, protective dome, encompasses all creation.

Do you grasp the monumental significance? Are you still unmoved by this momentous news?

The Almighty, unchanging and sovereign, governs all creation. His might is boundless, his purpose steadfast, his wisdom inscrutable).

This extraordinary volume unveils a treasure of God's sacred hymns prayer, heavenly secrets formerly concealed from the world. Unlike the complex practices of ages past, these heavenly inspired verses resonate powerfully with the modern spirit, echoing Christianity's shift from outward ritual to an intimate, *personal* communion with God, as Scripture itself reveals: These God's hymns embody a hidden wisdom — God's knowledge illuminating the pathway to a life brimming with miracles. I am a humble instrument, entrusted with a sacred legacy, a gift bestowed directly from a heavenly messenger, which I am sacred tasked to share with humanity. This secret wisdom — a rich tapestry woven from the threads of ages—offers an unparalleled bounty of spiritual illumination. It promises a sudden, breathtaking transformation, a glorious upheaval related to the transformational power of Pentecost, that life-altering event which ignited the apostles' ministry fifty days after Christ's resurrection.

Dispatched by God, a celestial messenger cloaked his true essence, existing in the world yet apart from it. His exceptional being, a paragon of enigma, resonated across Europe; a visible manifestation of God's influence that defied the constraints of chronology. Filled with infinite wisdom and an ageless soul—his superhuman attributes universally recognized—he surpassed the ephemeral boundaries of mortal existence. Only a few chosen brotherhoods sworn to secrecy, were entrusted with powerful, heaven-sent instruments of global redemption. These sacred artifacts and practices, veiled in impenetrable secrecy, remained jealously guarded within their exclusive order until destiny revealed their purpose. The world trembled on the precipice of annihilation; the rebellion surged, fanning the flames of revolution.

A being of celestial origin, comparable to the most revered spiritual icons, emanates a vibrant, violet healing radiance. This God's light, echoing the majesty and sanctity ascribed to Christ, wields transformative energy. Its influence surpasses the limitations of the physical and mental realms, reaching into the depths of the unconscious to dissolve ingrained, negative patterns. This luminescence functions as a restorative force, aligning the individual's innate, sacred core with its truest potential. Though remarkably similar in many respects in between Godsend with Christ', a difference separates them: one is the divine offspring, the other a heavenly messenger sent to our world. This celestial agent, filled with a sacred charge, played a role in assisting the Messiah for gathering a lost sheep in the European soil.

These sacred rites stood in stark contrast to the rituals of secret societies; Godsend' mission surpassed all earthly bonds. This gift from God Almighty is previously unknown comprehension of quantum power. The unparalleled simplicity of the Divine Secret Golden Hymns Prayer sets it apart. This concise invocation focuses solely on the Christ Light, yearning for a sacred, transformative merger with the divine. Its unique efficacy lies in fostering rapturous communion, instilling spiritual understanding, refining the soul into a vessel of grace, and unlocking the immense, latent power residing within its hallowed words. A Godsend-celestial being, veiled in secrecy, empowered a select cadre of twelve Knights Templar with a powerful, spiritual practice. This ascetic discipline, purged of all superfluous ritual, rejected ornate vestments and flamboyant displays. Its core was the introspective journey of the soul. Only the flickering torchlight, fragrant incense, and simple, ankle-length white hooded robes remained as tangible witnesses to this sacred work. Before embarking on this transformative undertaking, rigorous purification was absolutely essential.

Golden Hymns' sacred mysteries resonate with Christian traditions, revealing a nearly perfect alignment in principle and spiritual inclination. Its central doctrines are wholly dedicated to the intimate, transcendent Godhead—a singular, unifying truth echoing the figure of Christ—and the believer's communion with the Triune Deity. This intense emphasis on virtuous conduct and a life wholly devoted to God strikingly mirrors the Christian aspiration for redemption through a divine savior.

Christian piety and the practice of Divine Hymns resonate deeply, exhibiting striking parallels not merely in their inherent nature but also in their outward expressions. The congruity is evident in the reverent participation in sacred song, the meticulous recitation of scripture and holy texts and the commitment to righteous conduct permeating every facet of daily existence. In contrast, the Godsent' practices and displays were entirely free from ritual sacrifice or heathen beliefs. Their demonstrations, eschewing all embellishment and pomp, radiated an uncompromising simplicity. Moreover, the striking discrepancies in their pre-performance routines before engaging in their hallowed ritual, the participants' complete psycho-physical surrender unveiled disparities previously obscured. The ensuing predicament crystallized these differences with stark, illuminating clarity. This sacred, divinely bestowed practice demanded prayer and meticulously structured components sequenced as follows.

Following the celestial being's sacred mandate, the twelve consecrated Knights Templar, their preparations impeccably complete, then initiated the solemn supplication for the Almighty's ethereal grace. Through painstaking preparation, he cultivated an inner peace. His rigorous physical discipline—refined postures, deliberate stances, and controlled respiration—harmonized mind, body, and soul, achieving a singular devotion to the supreme being. Each month, under the cloak of midnight, their sacred ceremonies begin. A deep, contemplative journey follows, sparked by passionate prayers for mankind, overflowing with selfless affection. As the hours unfold, this transforms into a sacred devotion: a rich, interwoven unity of holy hymns—sung, intoned and whispered—each phrase a pause for deep reverential reflection.

Transformative self-discovery, the unveiling of one's true calling and the fulfillment of a preordained path—none of these aspirations are guaranteed solely by willpower, contrary to assertions prevalent in secular writings. While achievement might sometimes seem spontaneous and unlabored, true mastery invariably requires

God's intervention, a collaboration with a force beyond our comprehension. Despite widespread philosophical and religious exploration, a consensus on humanity's intrinsic link to a divine blueprint, preordained destiny, and a grand cosmic architecture remains frustratingly unattainable; faith in such an interconnectedness is notably scarce. While freedom reins in choosing our life's any ambition, however complex or simple, the achievement of our life's grand design is ultimately precarious. Many fail to grasp the divinely appointed chance for fulfillment, an opportunity missed when personal volition diverges from a preordained, transcendent path. Our liberty of choice, while absolute, does not guarantee the realization of destiny unless aligned with a higher, Godly orchestrated plan. Without access to a transcendent power, an ethereal understanding of our purpose, life becomes a protracted struggle. The connection between intention and outcome is severed; efforts yield no lasting fulfillment, leaving only a desolate void. Destiny's fulfillment demands an inner wisdom; otherwise, years are squandered in fruitless striving.

Unleashing phenomenal potential requires harnessing the potent energy of miraculous breakthroughs. God's intervention fuels this unstoppable momentum, showering the soul with blessings of amplified prosperity and transformative magnificence. This powerful concoction of spiritual insight and healing remedies rapidly alters existing circumstances, dissolving lifelong struggles and inaugurating an age of unprecedented affluence. The hymn's resonance acts as a powerful antidote, dissolving the insidious grip of ancestral curses. These dark triad afflictions, a complex inheritance woven into the very fabric of being, manifest as pervasive, multi-faceted challenges affecting mind, body, and soul. Unseen and often unrecognized, these karmic burdens lie dormant within the spirit, their subtle influence shaping the afflicted destiny.

Dark influences, born from unholy alliances or treacherous connections, can invade one's existence. These sinister bonds subtly inject destructive energies, often remaining imperceptible, insidiously permeating the very core of one's self. Deeply rooted malevolence — whether ancestral curses or demonic possessions —

constitutes a severe and unrelenting menace, clinging relentlessly to its prey and inflicting lasting, crippling afflictions. Humanity's deepest longing is for lasting happiness — a universal aspiration. Accessing this great joy requires more than mere wishing; it demands a conscious engagement with spiritual truth, much like the revelatory power within the Golden Hymns. This ancient wisdom, a wellspring of divine grace, unveils a path to unparalleled blessings, a potential so vast it transcends limitations. The transformational power released unlocks achievements previously deemed impossible, shattering barriers to a life overflowing with abundance. Embrace unwavering faith and a childlike trust in the boundless generosity of the Divine. This openness cultivates a heightened sensitivity, expanding your perception to encompass previously unimaginable horizons and a future radiant with limitless possibilities.

God's immense compassion, has bestowed upon humanity, a liberating truth in this age. Embrace this sacred wisdom; it's the key to unlocking an inherent potential and embarking on a triumphant journey of limitless growth, fulfilling divinely ordained destiny. The divine messenger proclaims:

"Unlock your inherent potential—a divinely ordained gift—through the sacred power of this Golden Hymns Prayer. This potent invocation guides you toward a fulfilling destiny, a tangible reality shaped by your deepest, unshakeable aspirations. The universe responds to your authentic yearning, provided your desires resonate with profound spiritual conviction. This alignment with the divine will unveil your birthright, regardless of your background or present situation. Unleashed potential, limitless and eternal, awaits you. Through an ancient, sacred wisdom, you'll ascend to a transcendent realm, a divine sanctuary brimming with unparalleled fulfillment and unwavering protection. This higher dimension, ordained for your journey, offers a pinnacle of existence, exceeding all earthly limitations." (Undertake a boundless voyage of exploration, triggering a transformation. Awakening innate holy spirit begins a sacred pilgrimage in three phases: A rebirth, a purification, finally culminating in a triumphant, final resurgence. This powerful, luminous plea unlocks a revitalizing force, internally

regenerating the spirit while externally remodeling the world This Godly force transcends the confines of the material world, unveiling the possibility of a previously inconceivable truth—a life once deemed unattainable. God's might transcend limitations, molding even deeply rooted injustices into a more equitable existence. Embark on a journey of God's wonders. This God's hymns prayer will illuminate and eternally protect the path to a sublime, spiritual awakening, God unveils its radiant truth).

Who Was the Godsend, Cloaked in Human Form?

Across the ages, the God's message resonates, a persistent echo in the human soul. His timeless wisdom, a sacred inheritance of compassion, continues to shape destinies and illuminate enduring verities. In the mid-18th century, a time of absolute monarchies, Heaven sent its emissary to Earth. This divine messenger, a being of celestial origin, embarked upon a mission that began with an incarnation—a descent into human form. Though his ethereal nature was veiled, his heavenly essence shone through from infancy, imbuing his every act with miraculous power. Gradually, his noble birth revealed itself, and he ascended into the European aristocracy, a radiant star illuminating the courts with surpassed magnificence. Possessing an unparalleled intellect that defied human comprehension, this enigmatic figure radiated brilliance. His wisdom, a breathtaking phenomenon, transcended all known limitations, achieving a level of sublime transcendence. This exceptional individual revolutionized scholarship, science, and governance, leaving an indelible mark on each field and instantly commanding worldwide acclaim.

An ethereal luminescence emanated from him, a visible power suggesting the ability to transmute the ordinary into the extraordinary. He possessed a breathtaking grace, an innate nobility of character and demeanor that commanded respect. His spirituality was unmistakable, a radiant testament to his spiritual ascension. His unearthly attributes were undeniable; a celestial heritage gifted him with capabilities far exceeding mortal limitations. Ironically, this heavenly envoy, a stark contrast to the conventional image of humble devotion, appeared as a supremely accomplished European, his exceptional qualities serving as the essential tools for his God ordained mission. Across ages and hemispheres, he was revered as the undying champion, his timeless presence a testament to humanity's unyielding spirit. His singular mission: to fiercely defend the inherent, God-given right to exist authentically, a life harmoniously aligned with one's deepest spiritual truth.

Biblical luminaries — prophets, angels, and the messianic Christ himself — manifest throughout both Testaments, their appearances often marked by a radiant, transformative light. This luminescence displayed a spectrum of vibrant hues: gold, purple, verdant green, the azure of turquoise, and jasper's multifaceted brilliance. Each color, imbued with symbolic weight, conveyed hierarchical rank, inherent attributes, and unique spiritual qualities. The revelation of these figures, however, was not uniformly accessible. For those blessed with a deep, ancestral spiritual heritage, God's light unveiled a richer, more nuanced understanding. Ultimately, these celestial beings appeared either to individuals chosen by God or, on grander occasions, to humanity as a whole, acting under divine decree.

Godsend' Essence and Role

Sent from the heavens on a sacred mission, a celestial being assumed human guise, dwelling amongst us mortals. Echoing narratives found in holy scriptures, this celestial being, like others before him, wore the mask of earthly birth, a shared human veneer. Yet, these ethereal messengers remained cloaked in an illusion, their godlike essence hidden beneath a deceptive veil of mortality. Only upon the triumphant completion of their heavenly tasks did their true nature—and the awesome might they commanded—become undeniably manifest. The Scripture bear witness to this fundamental truth.

"....There are also heavenly bodies and there are earthly bodies; but the splendor of the heavenly bodies is one kind, and the splendor of the earthly bodies is another. The sun has one kind of splendor, the moon another and the stars another; and star differs from star in splendor. So will it be with the resurrection of the dead. The body that is sown is perishable, it is raised imperishable; it is sown in dishonor, it is raised in glory; it is sown in weakness, it is raised in power; it is sown a

natural body, it is raised a spiritual body. If there is a natural body, there is also a spiritual body. So it is written: The first man Adam became a living being", the last Adam, a life-giving spirit. The spiritual did not come first, but the natural, and after that the spiritual. "The first man was of the dust of the earth; the second man is of heaven. As was the earthly man, so are those who are of the earth; and as is the heavenly man, so also are those who are of heaven. And just as we have borne the image of the earthly man, so shall we bear the image of the heavenly man. I declare to you, brother sand sisters, that flesh and blood can not inherit the kingdom of God, nor does the perishable inherit the imperishable. Listen, I tell you a mystery: We will not all sleep, but we will all be changed – in a flash, in the twinkling of an eye, at the last trumpet. For the trumpet will sound, the dead will be raised imperishable, and we will be changed. For the perishable must clothe itself with the imperishable and the mortal with immortality. When the perishable has been clothed with the imperishable, and the mortal with immortality, then the saying that is written will come true: "Death has been swallowed up in victory." "Where, O death, is your victory? Where,

O death, is your sing?" The sting of death is sin,
and the power of sin is the law. Be thanks be to
God! He gives us the victory through our Lord
*Jesus Christ.*₃ *(Celestial and terrestrial forms exist, each*
possessing a unique radiance. The sun's glory surpasses
the moon and the stars themselves vary in brilliance, a
dazzling spectrum of light. Similarly, the resurrection
will reveal a transformative splendor. What is sown
in mortality will rise in immortality; what is planted
in shame will bloom in majesty; weakness will yield
to awesome power; the physical will be transfigured
into the spiritual. The existence of a physical body
implies the reality of a spiritual one. Scripture reveals
this truth: Adam, the first man, received life; the last
Adam, Christ, bestows life everlasting. The spiritual
did not precede the physical; rather, it followed. The
first man was molded from earthly dust; the second, a
celestial being, descended from heaven. Earthly beings
reflect the nature of the earthly man, while heavenly
beings mirror the divine. As we now bear the likeness
of the earthly Adam, we shall inherit the likeness of the
heavenly Christ. My brothers and sisters, understand
this mystery: mortal flesh cannot claim God's kingdom;
the perishable cannot inherit immortality. Listen closely:

---

3.   1Corinthians 15:40-58 1 Corinthians 15:40-58

a glorious transformation awaits us—a breathtaking, instantaneous metamorphosis at the final trumpet call. The trumpet will sound, the deceased will rise in incorruptible bodies, and we, the living, will be transformed. The mortal must don immortality; decay must yield to everlasting life. When this union is complete, the prophetic words will find fulfillment: "Death is vanquished!" Death, where is your triumph? Death, where is your sting? Sin is the venom of death; the law empowers sin's dominion. But praise God, who grants us victory through Christ).

A miraculous intervention, emerging in the heart of 18th-century Europe. This enigmatic figure, allegedly to be the offspring of the illustrious Prince Francis Rakoczi II, heir to the Transylvanian throne, a lineage of power and legacy was purportedly his birthright, however a legacy lies shrouded in persistent ambiguity, its true nature forever elusive. Even in childhood, Saint Germain exhibited an otherworldly brilliance, a luminous prodigy whose intellect eclipsed all contemporaries. His exceptional gifts were evident from the start, a radiant manifestation of extraordinary genius. His mastery extended across a vast expanse of disciplines, demonstrating a mature understanding rarely witnessed. Effortlessly, he acquired fluency in twenty languages, achieving excellence in virtually every scholarly pursuit. His exceptional talents eclipsed those of his contemporaries, a breathtaking display of intellectual might that hinted at an astonishingly powerful mind. He dedicated himself to exploring the intricate interplay between faith and reason.[4]

Godsend's arrival, shrouded in mystery, initiated a profound and enduring legacy. His transcendent departure only amplified the enigmatic impact of his earthly sojourn. A life punctuated by momentous acts, his ministry remains a vibrant, transformative force, its influence indelibly etched upon the fabric of our existence.

His return to the highest echelons of power transformed his existence into a continent-spanning sensation. Though not acknowledged as a celestial being, the mysterious Count St. Germain—a European prodigy whose genius shone incandescently propelled him across national borders on countless vital missions. A

---

4.   Manly P. Hall, Saint-Germain

revolutionary figure instantly welcomed by two powerful factions: the monarchy's innermost circle and simultaneously, a clandestine brotherhood of Europe's foremost scientific luminaries. Within the hidden world of secret societies, this pivotal figure in the genesis of European secret organizations, served as their enigmatic director. Their groundbreaking advancements in modern Judeo-Christian Hermeticism served as a deceptive façade, masking the truly sublime aspirations that drove their cryptic inquiries. Driven by intense experimentation and fervent mysticism, he relentlessly guided these societies toward illumination. Following a cosmic roadmap and the accumulated wisdom of their fraternity, their unwavering pursuit aimed at unveiling the universe's deepest secrets. However, these occurrences were but a cunning illusion, masking the transcendent, preordained design at their heart.

The Complex bond with Louis XV

Masquerading as Saint Germain, a celestial envoy forged a powerful bond with Louis XV, gaining immediate access to the king's inner circle. This divine agent, simultaneously spearheaded a formidable network: the preeminent brotherhood of European occult organizations.

His exceptional qualities elevated him to a position of significant power and influence within the court of Louis XV, making him a singular figure of note.[5] While Saint Germain's paramount objective was international negotiation, his engagements were frequently entangled with King Louis XV's clandestine investigations. The King's covert inquiries focused on unearthing the concealed political machinations and territorial ambitions of neighboring monarchs. Through his covert operations for the monarchy, he gained immense power and prestigious social connections, effortlessly acquiring all the resources necessary for his sacred undertaking. Sadly, the cataclysmic upheaval obliterated most of his irreplaceable

---

5. Manly P. Hall, Saint-Germain

work, leaving behind only the desolate remnants of vital documentation.

During a profound spiritual pilgrimage, Saint Germain's guidance led me on a captivating quest across France, retracing his illustrious steps. My journey culminated in the discovery of a single, publicly accessible testament to his existence, a poignant relic preserved by the French state. Within the majestic Château de Chambord, I found the enduring imprint of his presence. His apartment, situated on the second floor's northern wing, commands a significant position, directly aligned with the chateau's central axis and remarkably close to the King's own quarters. A striking portrait, prominently displayed near his chamber's entrance, bears the inscription *"Comte de Saint Germain, a Celebrated Man,"* a testament to the regal favor bestowed upon him: *"This apartment was a gift from King Louis XV."*

Godsend' Handwritten Manuscripts

In an era of absolute monarchs, heaven's messenger's holy mission remained obscured; the appointed hour had not yet arrived. These brethren, mirroring their Judeo-Christian counterparts, yearned for the same transcendent prize: Eternal life-immortality. The crucial distinction lay in their clandestine methods; they sought God's apotheosis, eternal existence unmediated by Christ. This era of imperial sway saw the emergence of a celestial envoy, a figurehead who rose to unparalleled prominence among the intellectual elite of secret societies. His aura commanded absolute reverence, a palpable testament to otherworldly power subtly shaping terrestrial affairs.

A central figure among Europe's spiritual luminaries, he revealed eight sacred scriptures. These transformative, largely clandestine texts contained an insight into humanity's spiritual evolution—A transformative journey to eradicate societal evils and conquer base instincts, ultimately ushering in a radiant rebirth of humanity's potential. These writings functioned as a vital key, deciphering his subsequent works and charting a course through his complex endeavors. Rooted in a Judeo-Christian framework, their fundamental beliefs are shaped by a potent blend of philosophical and spiritual currents, inextricably interwoven with the mystical tapestry of Kabbalah. An arcane, Jewish mystical tradition, originally transmitted through whispered secrets and cloaked in cryptic ciphers, offers a symbolic framework for interpreting sacred biblical texts.

During a resurgence of cryptic spiritual wisdom, culminating in the medieval period and impacting Hasidism, God's teachings stressed His pervasive presence throughout creation. This emphasis underscored the imperative to perpetually connect with, and ultimately merge with God. The core of religious observance became fervent devotion, while even physicality and everyday actions were imbued with spiritual significance.

Ancient initiation rituals, rich with divine wisdom, found meticulous record in elaborate texts and evocative iconography. These artifacts powerfully encapsulated timeless, universal verities. Central to this legacy stands the revered

"Pymander," a seventeen-part collection of fragmented scriptures. Their interwoven layers – secret codes, enigmatic symbols, hieroglyphic illustrations and archaic dialects – constitute an enduring influence. This seminal work has served for centuries as an indispensable guide for initiates, spiritual guides and visionary minds. Hidden within an intentionally perplexing cipher — letters reversed, reflected and encrypted using esoteric alphabets — lie cosmic truths, jealously guarded from the profane. Numerical data is either conspicuously omitted or subtly concealed through an intricate web of codes, glyphs and enigmatic symbols protecting sacred lore from the unworthy gaze. Only those possessing dominion over otherworldly entities and infernal powers can unravel the universe's limitless, celestial power.

The celestial being, St. Germain's manuscripts are distinguished by these remarkable titles:[6]

> *The Saint; Company of God;*
> *The Sacred Attribute;*
> *Mystery Unveiled;*
> *The Great Sage and Divine Pymander;*

---

6. Manly P. Hall. The most holy trinosophia of the Comte de St. Germain.

Holy Science: Divine Supernatural;
The Ring of the Fire;
The Saint, Sage and Seers;
The Most Holy Wisdom.

A hidden legacy of esoteric knowledge, meticulously guarded by brilliant minds within Europe's secret societies and deeply perceptive spiritual seekers from diverse backgrounds sprang from ancient scriptures. This arcane wisdom circulated both alongside and after the purported arrival of its God's source. Lost to the annals of history, two sacred texts inexplicably revealed amidst the tumultuous upheaval of the French Revolution, vanished utterly from the custodians' grasp.

God's Providence

Judeo-Christian thought, a potent blend of religious conviction and philosophical inquiry, served as a symbolic lexicon for spiritual truths. Its core narrative depicted a metamorphosis: the arduous ascent from a state of earthly, shadowed existence – a consciousness weighed down by the material – to a being radiant with spiritual enlightenment. This journey, central to the faith, involved a meticulous purification of body, mind and spirit, driven by an intense focus on inner processes. Before unveiling the celestial being's sacred, ultimate design to its civilization, a foundational, preliminary revelation of divine origin served as a crucial, initial step. Christ's divine spark ignites a soul-altering journey. This sacred mission sourced in the ultimate mystery, cultivates the God within, fostering a growth that culminates in eternal union with the Alpha and Omega. The goal: perfect communion with God, a blessed immortality. The opportune unveiling of the Golden Hymns Prayer's diving secret to those two powerful civilizations was tragically thwarted by the French Revolution's upheaval. This irretrievable loss silenced the sacred knowledge, shrouding it in secrecy except for a select few: the twelve Knights Templar, those valiant soldiers of Christ and the Temple of Solon. Thus, this God's mystery remains a guarded inheritance, its truth concealed until this very day.

A chasm separated the divinely ordained purpose, a gift of grace from the self-proclaimed salvation sought by the intellectual elite of that era. Both factions, however, yearned for redemption; one found it in God's boundless mercy, the other in the purported might of the human intellect. Rooted in the complex currents of ancient Alexandria, the secret society's creed emerged from a unique blend of philosophy and religion. This sophisticated system posited that enlightenment, a path to salvation, could be achieved solely through rigorous intellectual pursuit and the skillful application of sacred knowledge. Experimentation, guided by wisdom, constituted the core of this self-directed journey to spiritual liberation, rejecting the need for any external redeemer or messianic figure. A celestial entity, patiently awaiting the opportune moment, concealed his divine purpose. He prepared to infuse the sacred essence of CORE (Christ) into the highest echelons of society; his heavenly mandate shrouded in secrecy. The sacred, golden litany – a prayer of inherent power – remained unheard by the two dominant cultures; the auspicious time for its revelation had yet to dawn. France's revolutionary upheaval unleashed widespread turmoil, irrevocably shattering the existing religious order. The ascendance of a deistic cult marked the decisive eclipse of traditional divine belief.[7]

Ancient Egyptian arcane knowledge known as Khemia, underwent a transformation during the Greek conquest, morphing into al-Khemia under Arab rule. The origins of this discipline, however, remain shrouded in mystery. The catastrophic destruction of the Alexandrian Library—an unparalleled repository of learning— irrevocably erased a vast amount of its historical record, leaving scholars to grapple with great ambiguities and persistent uncertainties regarding its venerable past.[8] In the eighth century, an influx of ancient wisdom, transmitted by Arab scholars

7. The Oxford History of the French Revolution
8. Alison M. Roberts. Hathor's Alchemy: The ancient Egyptian Roots of the Hermetic art

into the Iberian Peninsula, ignited a transformative wave across Europe and beyond. This esoteric knowledge, captivating the intellectual elite, fostered a clandestine fraternity dedicated to the resurgence of a sacred, mystical tradition. Its dissemination became a phenomenon, quickly captivating those with refined intellect and spiritual yearning. Secluded in mountainous regions, these revered sages—initially hermits— cultivated practices of contemplation and healing. These methods yielded transformative spiritual insights, fueling their quest for eternal life, an unending existence beyond mortality's grasp.

A hidden legacy, guarded by a select few, blossomed into a sophisticated exploration of spiritual and alchemical processes. These investigations eventually found their way into conventional healing practices, giving rise to a unique and venerable system of Oriental medicine. This esoteric discipline involves recitation of seventy-two God's names, employing potent thaumaturgy and deciphering cryptic scriptures to unlock miraculous abilities. Herbal remedies, meditative states, and the induction of altered consciousness synergistically awaken the latent psycho-physical potential, unleashing the divine forces and the quest for eternal life. Sacred purple, a hue signifying the divine, embodied spirituality, restorative power and celestial guardianship. Their practice relied on invoking this sacred light to draw forth healing grace. Driven by a devout, almost mystical faith in their scientific pursuits, these revered scholars sought the elusive prize of immortality, independent of any messianic intervention. This ambition, deeply ingrained and fervently held, constituted their ultimate aspiration.

Gold, a pivotal element in their methodology, held significance. Its radiant hue embodied God's link, representing the apex of chromatic splendor. For these sacred practitioners, gold's unparalleled purity and majestic aura served as both emblem and essence, a cornerstone of their practice. It embodies potent authority, enduring success, abundant wealth and a spiritual metamorphosis. Representing purity, knowledge, and insightful comprehension, it embodies the radiant jewel of spiritual awakening, a beacon illuminating the path to truth. Within the Judeo-Christian theological framework, the crucible of fire elevates gold and crimson, forging them into potent symbols of spiritual illumination. Throughout history, revered scholars have viewed gold's intrinsic nature as a celestial bridge, a conduit connecting the earthly realm to the divine, inextricably linked to the ultimate achievement, the Magnum Opus.

Culminating the Judeo-Christian metamorphosis - Individual transformation towards God within a Judeo-Christian framework - the legendary Philosopher's Stone—a potent elixir of eternal life—unleashes its God's power, bestowing boundless rejuvenation and conferring immortality. This ultimate achievement represents the apex of perfection, a radiant apotheosis and the attainment of celestial serenity. The recondite knowledge-hidden from most people- whispered through the ages, lies encrypted within the cryptic acronym V.I.T.R.I.O.L. Descend into the earth's depths; through rigorous refinement, the philosopher's stone hidden and elusive, shall be revealed to the diligent seeker. The Philosopher's Stone *(the elixir of life)*, however served as the secret *(sealed)* tradition's paramount emblem, embodying the transformative journey toward Christ-like apotheosis. These authors united in their conviction, championed the spiritual enrichment promised by artistic dedication, vigilantly safeguarding the sanctity of God's law and sacred knowledge from the corrupting influence of authority. Myths and legends whisper of a cosmic secret: the universe's potent energy entrusted to humanity's core lies dormant, it's awesome might carefully veiled within the human spirit.

PART II

God's Decree and Promise

"For the Lord Gives wisdom; from his mouth come knowledge and understanding." [1]

(God's infinite wisdom is the origin of all understanding, a gift bestowed with boundless grace).

---

1. Proverbs 2:6

God's Law of Destiny

The Scripture prevailed in every continent and influenced and formed a new religious-cultural norma; there are similar wisdom anecdotes are available since the time immemorial. It suggests that humans possess significant inner potential that can be expressed in the external world. In the verse speaks of being strengthened with power through the Spirit in the inner being: inner strength that comes from a divine source.[2] Furthermore, God is "able to do exceedingly abundantly above all that is asked or thought, according to the power that works in us."[3] It implies that there is a vast, even unlimited, power within believers that can achieve remarkable things. Another verse states: "I can do all things through Christ who strengthens me."[4] It highlights the power granted to believers through faith, enabling them to overcome challenges and a achieve what might seem impossible on their own.

---

2. Ephesians 3:16
3. Ephesians 3:20
4. Philippians 4:13

"There is or can be a winner inside: leaders, thinkers, or artists; there are dreams and desires, and needs. We are that being, uniquely called to occupy a precise place in the cosmic order no matter where or in what era we live. Everyone possesses that potential within; it can be reached that particular being through the divine wisdom and manifested in the outer world."[5] (*Within every person resides a latent potential for greatness — leader, thinker, or artist; Our deepest longings and fundamental requirements shape the very core of our being; our common humanity springs from a fundamental, inherited architecture – a potent legacy of ancestral learning and lived experience, passed down through the ages. Our inherent capabilities, kindled by passionate longing, manifest in individual destinies, exceeding all temporal and geographical limitations; we are born with ingrained behavioral predispositions, powerful primordial images that an influence our actions. These inherent patterns of conduct, echoing across generations, constitute a pre-existing spiritual matrix that molds our lives. Inner greatness awaits God's inspiration unlocks its brilliance*).

---

5. Ancient wisdom: Unknown

God's plan fills each existence with a unique, consecrated purpose, a predetermined destiny unfolding on this mortal coil. The Scriptures powerfully declare this innate blueprint, unveiling a Godly ordained path for each existence:

"Before I formed you in the womb I knew you, before you were born, I set you apart; I appointed you...."[6] *(Before your birth, I set you apart for a holy calling. I destined you for this, and I remain your steadfast protector).*

"The Lord has made everything for his own purposes, even the wicked for a day of disaster."[7] *(A preordained cosmic plan shaped all existence, deliberately fashioning even the wicked for a final, devastating judgment).*

Our lives may be scripted, a celestial blueprint etched into our very being, a predetermined trajectory inherent in this transient existence. This immutable path, possibly encrypted within our DNA, silently yearns for its revelation.

We face an undeniable reality, a truth as vast and unwavering as the universe itself. To

---

6. Jeremiah 15
7. Proverbs 16: 4

disregard this inherent, inescapable path is to invite a devastating loss of direction, a shattering of inner equilibrium, leaving the individual adrift in the turbulent currents of existence. This turbulent maelstrom of doubt and discord can ensnare individuals in an extended period of upheaval. Alternatively, they may remain stagnant, adrift in a sea of purposelessness, battling a complex tapestry of psychological, somatic, spiritual, and emotional suffering, potentially leading to self-harm.

The steadfast refusal of Christ reveals an inherent spiritual malady. Consequently, dismissing God's guidance casts the individual into a bleak, desolate emptiness, a barren landscape of apathy and anguish. This isolating alienation deprives them of grace's redemptive potential, leaving them utterly vulnerable and hopelessly lost to salvation's embrace. To deny one's fundamental nature is to commit self-treachery, sacrificing the very foundations of personal fulfillment. This disavowal condemns one to a bleak and barren existence, a life stripped of meaning and vitality, spiraling inexorably towards decay.

Plato envisioned a perfect, unalterable geometric design — the archetype — as the bedrock of reality, an eternal and inviolable truth. This immutable, sacred edict dictates existence, demanding allegiance that transcends mortality. Our seemingly chaotic lives, a collection of disjointed fragments, ultimately unveil a magnificent, overarching pattern: God's plan often veiled from our conscious awareness. This inherent, flawless structure, a testament to God's artistry, compels us toward a deeper understanding of our place within its intricate design.

This sacred journey, divinely appointed, necessitates an immersion in life's interwoven tapestry. A grand, preordained design guarantees ultimate success, culminating in a reward of such sublime beauty it surpasses comprehension. Celestial grace saturates this regal path, divinely protected and relentlessly guarded. Providence unfolds with effortless ease, a multitude of benevolent helpers propelled by an unstoppable, exhilarating force. Holy scriptures reveal a transcendental truth: unwavering commitment to this principle is paramount:

"I am the true vine, and my Father is the vine-grower. He removes every branch in me that bears no fruit. Every branch that bears fruit he prunes to make it bear more fruit." [1] *(I am the life-source, nurtured by my Father, the ultimate cultivator. He prunes away the barren, but cultivates the righteous branches, ensuring a greater harvest of virtue.).*

Obstacles—people, things, and unfavorable circumstances—that hinder your advancement will be swiftly and decisively purged by a beneficent power. This cleansing action creates space for growth, nurturing the flourishing potential within you. Through this meticulous cultivation, a trust in the cosmos's generative force blossoms. Consequently, unproductive desires fade, supplanted by ambitions harmoniously aligned with a transcendent purpose.

This momentous decision, a catalyst for metamorphosis, initiates a crucial turning point. The ensuing transformation, a breathtaking passage demands resilience and fortitude, ultimately leading you to a critical juncture—the threshold of your epic endeavor. This reality deviates drastically from

---

1. John 15:1-2

your envisioned path, an unsettling and abhorrent ordeal. Sweeping transformations are imminent, ushering in an era of an inspiring upheaval. To fully grasp the momentous implications of this epochal shift, let the luminous, sacred verses of the divine Hymns prayer illuminate your soul through daily contemplation.

Across millennia, sages have consistently urged adherence to intuitive guidance; true wisdom then unfolds organically. This undeniable, celestial prompting—an inner knowing, a human experience—serves as infallible God's direction. For those receptive to the divine whisper, immense possibilities unfold. This extraordinary endowment, the very core of our existence, is humanity's most precious inheritance. Trust in a higher power to orchestrate your life's trajectory, rather than relying solely on rational planning. Inspiration's powerful essence hinges upon the pillars of sagacity, erudition, and insight. Sacred texts unveil a fundamental truth:

"For the Lord gives wisdom; from his mouth come knowledge and understanding." [2] *(Divine*

---

2. Proverbs 2:6

providence bestows profound insight; from the Almighty's pronouncements flow enlightenment and discernment). Moreover, sacred texts illuminate the prophet's understanding of divinely bestowed wisdom's potent influence:

"And your ears shall hear a word behind you, saying, 'This is the way, walk in it...God speaks to us through our intuition, guiding us in the right direction. When we listen attentively, we can discern His voice leading us on the right path." [3] *(A gentle whisper will echo in your consciousness, a subtle guidance murmuring, "This is the path; follow it." Divine intuition, an inner knowing, serves as God's compass, steering us toward our destined course. By cultivating mindful awareness, we unlock the capacity to decipher His subtle promptings, and thus, confidently traverse the righteous way).*

Transcending the rigid framework of logic and reason, a universe unfolds, defying clear articulation. To unlock your inherent divinity through a quantum lens requires a commitment to essential foundations. Navigating your destined path necessitates focus; only through dedication

---

3. Isaiah 30:21

will enlightenment dawn. Sacred texts, repositories of ageless knowledge, issue a stark warning: Embrace this guidance with resolve:

"Do not turn back,"[4] *(Press onward; doubt is your enemy. Relentless pursuit is crucial; straying is fatal)*

"Do not turn to the right or the left; keep your foot from evil"[5] *(Resist the alluring whispers of vice; reject evil resolutely, and diligently follow the path of virtue).*

"... do not lose sight of these-keep sound wisdom and discretion."[6] *(Always exercise sound judgment and wisdom- Cultivate insightful discernment and astute decision-making in all endeavors. Prioritize a considered, sagacious approach, consistently evaluating implications and acting with deliberation).*

"Tell no one." *(Maintain absolute secrecy. This strategy demands complete discretion. Let the knowledge remain confined to your own guarded heart. Silence is paramount; its preservation is critical).* Obsession with yesteryear hinders our spiritual growth, a truth echoed in sacred scriptures. Solomon's

---

4. Genesis 19:17
5. Proverbs 4:27
6. Proverbs 3:21-25

wisdom urges his descendants toward resolution, a persistent pursuit of God's knowledge. A celestial revelation unveils a powerful secret: mask your ambitions, cloaking them in careful reticence. This subtle, yet transformative tactic unleashes dormant capabilities, revealing a path to unimaginable power.

Sacred texts unveil God's enduring gifts. We must diligently explore these revelations, embracing their transformative power:

"Go and tell no one."[7] *(This intelligence requires the strictest confidentiality. Its concealment is of critical importance).*

"And He charged him to tell no one,..."[8] *(He strictly prohibited revealing the vital secret)*

"See that you tell no one..."[9] *(This plan must remain utterly confidential. Disclosure would trigger a devastating chain of events; its inviolability is paramount).*

Christ's sublime, whispered injunction to seek serenity holds a sacred import beyond

---

7. Mark 1
8. Luke 5:14
9. Matthew 8:4

human grasp. Across cultures, a deep-seated reluctance to prematurely disclose one's ambitions is evident; this widespread sagacity highlights the immense value of carefully guarded intentions. See the significant examples below for a clearer understanding.

"Never tell anyone your goals...let the results reveal by itself."[10] *(Let your successes be your testament; let your achievements speak for themselves).*

"Keeping your goals in your heart may help you to achieve them."[11] *(Intense desires pave the way to ultimate fulfillment).*

"Don't tell anyone what you are attempting to achieve until it's finished. External potency can cast off goals."[12] *(Conceal your aspirations until they mature; premature exposure jeopardizes their inherent momentum).*

"Many aspirations subside or fades away because they are shared with the wrong people..."[13] *(Many*

---

10. Unanimous
11. Unanimous
12. Unanimous
13. Unknown

noble aspirations crumble into dust, stifled by ill-judged confidences bestowed upon unworthy recipients).

"If you want to live a happy life, tie it to a goal, not to people or things."[14] *(True fulfillment stems from a life purpose, not fleeting pleasures).*

Ancient Greek eminent philosophers explored the implications of absolute secrecy, transcending its conventional interpretation. Stoicism cultivates inner resilience through introspection, fostering serenity and lasting change. This tranquility, the cornerstone of genuine growth, empowers decisive action toward your life's purpose. Nurture your aspirations; self-discovery demands immediate commitment:

"Ancient philosophers of stoic tradition reveal that a personal transformational experience is wise to be kept private, allowing them to intensify the strength within the self. They thought us to retain our holy grail to ourselves, not only by virtue of secrecy but also nurturing, maintaining the self-mastery, while embrace the peace from concealment. This is to amour one's peace of mind, serenity to advance the

14. Albert Einstein: the quote

true clout, applying a reticence and wisdom as an influence for a catalysts or modification, transformation; bringing the genuine principle, lifeblood of existing tracing pilgrimage. It's a moment to evolve, widen, and bound, enhancing the existence fundamentally that will provide a profound impact. The genuine clout is originated in a tranquil sector of life. Thus, they encourage us not to wait any longer for our destined path (Divine Calling). "Now is the time to get serious about your ultimate goals...Don't share your convictions. How long can you afford to put off who you really are? Your nobler self cannot wait any longer."[15] (Stoic sages understood the power of solitary introspection. A transformative journey, they believed, flourishes best in the quietude of self-reflection, its potency amplified by the deliberate absence of external validation. This transformative process, this revelation, requires vigilant protection — *not merely cloaked in secrecy, but carefully cultivated, nurtured as a testament to self-discipline, its tranquility born from deliberate concealment. Cultivating inner tranquility and composure strengthens genuine influence, employing*

---

15. Epictetus The Enchiridion, 125 BCE, Greece. 1683 AD, Ch. 1.

discretion and sagacity to catalyze positive change and transformation. This fosters the vital essence of a meaningful life, a journey of self-discovery and purposeful growth. This is a pivotal juncture for transformative growth, expansion, and advancement, enriching our lives in ways that resonate deeply. True power springs from the serene corners of our being. Therefore, let us embrace our destined trajectory—our God's purpose—without further delay. The moment demands unwavering commitment to your loftiest aspirations. Conceal your deepest beliefs. How much longer will you tolerate the chasm between your true essence and your present reality? Your superior nature yearns for liberation; delay no further).

Their core philosophy, a powerful blend of quiet diligence and resounding achievement, advocates for persistent, silent effort; let success speak volumes.

Consequently, spiritual insight counsels against the use of caustic language, contemptuous barbs, and any form of social denigration; lest we invite a reciprocal onslaught of negativity into our own lives. Minimizing worldly entanglements preserves the inner reservoir of God's power. Ancient scriptures unveil a core tenet, a sacred duty demanding our unwavering devotion: This path requires diligent introspection and dedication:

"Anyone who hears my words and obeys them is like a wise man who reaches the high ground. But anyone who hears them and does not obey them is like a foolish man who forever stumbles ending in regret and sorrow."[16] *(Heeding my advice shows wisdom; ignoring it, folly. The wise build on solid ground; the foolish, on shifting sand, facing ruin and regret).*

"The Son is the image of the invisible God, the firstborn over all creation. For in Him all things were created: things in heaven and on earth, visible and invisible, whether thrones or powers or rulers or authorities; all things have been created through him and for Him. He is before all things, and in Him all things hold together."[17] *(Aligning ourselves with God's grants limitless blessings. Christ, the perfect expression of God, is the source of all creation, visible and unseen. All things exist through Him, for His glory; He is the eternal foundation of the universe).*

---

16. Matthew 7:24-25
17. Colossians 1:15-17

By accessing the universe's limitless potential, we unlock an infinite source of power, accomplishing incredible transformation. Pursuing the intricate, deceptive paths of reason as to the pursuit of a fantastical ideal or blind devotion to ancestral blueprints, such as rigidly defined family paths, frequently results in agonizing stagnation; however, the true wisdom arises from courageous faith and the surrender of self-direction. The central tenets of this ancient creed are revealed in the foundational principles detailed below:

"There are warriors, kings or sages in myself, to be a warrior in the outer world, one must be a warrior in the inner world; to be a king in the outer world, one must be a king in the inner world; to be a sage in the outer world, one must be a sage in the inner world."[18] *(Heroism, kingship, and enlightenment spring from inner strength, self-mastery, and profound self-knowledge. Courage breeds champions, self-rule creates leaders, and introspection yields wisdom).*

Surrendering to the inevitable unleashes a hidden reservoir of power, igniting a transformative

---

18. Anonymous

journey towards remarkable success. By fostering a contemplative spirit, open to the wisdom welling up from within, you become a conduit for God' grace. Inner tranquility dramatically enhances the influx of cosmic energy, empowering you to fulfill your sacred purpose with unparalleled effectiveness-abandon the relentless battle; lay down your defenses. Only then will you transcend the fruitless cycle of endless strife, escaping the meager rewards and disappointment that inevitably follow. Divine generosity alone bestows gifts of unsurpassed perfection, immaculate in every detail. Only the supremely merciful, all-powerful God can offer such unparalleled bounty.

Legends portray the hero's journey as an unfaltering pilgrimage undertaken by a solitary figure, their resolve adamantine, their vision fixed, and their dedication absolute. This transformative quest will forge an evolution, stripping away the limitations of their former existence to reveal a being of extraordinary power. Persistent adherence to a noble life will lead to spiritual enlightenment and a boundless realm of divine prosperity. Their arduous journey culminated in a glorious victory, formed in the crucible of spiritual awakening. Returning to the critical nexus, the hero confronts the exact point of origin, the fateful crossroads that launched their momentous and transformative journey. Returning to the critical nexus, the hero confronts the exact point of origin, the fateful crossroads that launched their momentous and transformative journey. Genuine victory necessitates a deep inner transformation, a symbolic death giving way to a spiritual rebirth of extraordinary power. While sometimes grounded in historical events, the epic tales of heroes don't play out in the ordinary realm; instead, they unfold within the vibrant, otherworldly theaters of the subliminal mind where powerful symbolism reigns supreme. Finally, the unconquerable will is broken, unleashing latent powers that yearn to reshape the world. This victory elevates being beyond the abyss of devastation, freeing it from its suffocating burden.

Discovering your inherent, God's ordained purpose is a deeply arduous journey, a complex and intricate pilgrimage whose final destination remains uncertain, yet rewarding. Increased vitality fosters a heightened receptiveness in the conscious mind, making it permeable to intuitive understandings. Consequently, direction floods the intellect, enriching it with invaluable knowledge, illuminating optimal life choices and their precise timing. Dismissing the quiet whispers of your inner wisdom, the soul's fervent longing remains unfulfilled, obscuring the vital truths that desperately seek expression. A hidden destiny, a priceless secret veiled in perplexing mystery, eludes persistent discovery. Winning the ultimate reward demands a deep, introspective odyssey. You must achieve a metamorphosis, becoming the very embodiment of your soul – your inherent, divine core. For those who bravely undertake this momentous journey of self-discovery, God's light will illuminate the path to inner revelation.

Embracing your life's purpose grants an unshakeable conviction; you walk a path of destiny, Godly appointed, each step resonant with Significance. A joy and deep satisfaction fill your life, erasing all traces of meaninglessness and despair. A powerful, compassionate God presence perpetually watches over you, deflecting negativity and malevolent influences. Your rapid advancement facilitates the seamless and highly effective accomplishment of your tasks and goals. Daily struggles now yield to your unwavering commitment; a spirit forged in the fires of perseverance renders past jealousies insignificant. Legend holds that the celestial azure bird imparts secrets to those receptive to its ethereal voice. Departing from God's blueprint yields a starkly contrasting existence, a far cry from the idealized state previously envisioned. Your present trajectory is devoid of a determined pursuit of significant goals, thereby jeopardizing the efficacy of your endeavors and potentially rendering them utterly fruitless.

Secret Path to Victory

Every individual possesses a singular, extraordinary talent, a precious endowment from a higher power. Tapping into your inherent brilliance fosters an intense, laser-like concentration, harmonizing mind and heightening perception, thereby generating extraordinary impactful achievements. However, this magnificent endowment can quickly diminish if yield to the insidious creep of doubt, unbelief, letting its venomous tendrils poison your soul. This innate capacity fosters unwavering confidence, driving the resolute transformation of ambitious dreams into decisive action. a boundless wellspring of potential capable of shaping reality itself. This awesome power, a gift from the heavens, grants us the terrifying capacity for creation and annihilation. To access this potent inner force, this sacred spark, we must first penetrate its hidden depths. Ancient texts reveal the keys to unlocking this extraordinary power: unyielding courage, tranquil acceptance, and an unshakeable faith in our inherent destiny for greatness. Only then can we fulfill our divinely ordained potential.

"Be strong! Be fearless! Don't be afraid and don't be scared by your enemies, because the LORD YOUR God is the one who marches with you"[19] *(Courage and resolute spirit are your armor. Let no foe intimidate you, for the Almighty marches at your side, a companion in the face of adversity.)*

At the root of all misery lies the profound torment of powerlessness. We often overlook the inherent, God-given strength residing within us, a strength whose absence is the genesis of all despair: *"All unhappiness comes from lack of power."*[20] *(Misery stems from powerlessness).*

People often dissipate their precious reserves of mental, physical, and emotional strength chasing fleeting goals, constructing fragile edifices upon unstable foundations. Their obsessive pursuit of transient worldly pleasures blinds them to their potential, leaving them spiritually impoverished and tragically unfulfilled. This fundamental precept is echoed in the rich tapestry of narratives from ancient societies worldwide, showcasing its timeless

---

19. Deuteronomy 31:6
20. Leo Tolstoy, War and Peace, Book 15, Ch.17 Marxists Internet Archive

validity. The Scripture unveils a striking dichotomy:

"...a time to be silent and a time to speak..." [21] (*Times for silent contemplation, and times that necessitate impassioned proclamation*).

"A few words are silver, but silence is gold." [22] (Silent contemplation, a priceless gem exceeding any speech, conveys immeasurable meaning).

A deep connection with the divine essence pulls you inexorably into the Almighty's world. Bathed in the Creator's limitless, resplendent majesty, one becomes a witness to wonders springing forth from the very wellspring of infinite existence.

The scripture echoes the aforementioned concept, a passage powerfully proclaiming a remarkable correspondence:

"God created man in His own image, in the image of God He created him; male and female He reacted them." [23] (*The God's hand, in its masterful creation, created humankind in His image, male and female,*

---

21. Ecclesiastes 3:7
22. Ancient anonymous
23. Genesis 1:27

the magnificent expression of His ingenuity was a testament to boundless creative force).

Reflecting the universe's sublime architecture, we are miniature replicas of God, intricately woven into its magnificent tapestry, a fundamental, inherent essence of Him—a sacred center—lies at the heart of existence; a mere semblance of celestial being is utterly inadequate. The Genesis account of God, the divine architect who fashioned humanity—*created him; male and female He reacted them*—presents an enduring mystery, endlessly interpreted and reimagined across cultures and throughout history. This concept's most captivating element, however lies in its implication of spiritual link between the mortal and immortal. This direct affinity signifies that whatever we do in the physical world will reflect itself in the spiritual world; ultimately, it can be achieved to be there is no division between heaven and earth through God's intelligence.

Recognizing our intrinsic connection to the higher spirit unveils a fundamental kinship between humankind and the divine's very being. We are not simply imitations of a divine archetype; instead, we are incandescent expressions of a sacred, indwelling light. Our unique, radiant spark—a sublime gift—sets us apart, lifting us to a higher plane of existence and empowering our collaboration with God in the creation of all things. We are not mere faint replicas of a transcendent intellect; rather, we are glorious manifestations, intrinsically woven into the God's design. The existence of life itself powerfully demonstrates the boundless creative capacity and sustaining force of a divine mind. By striving to grasp and manifest our inherent God's essence, we form a spiritual connection, creating a life of earthly paradise. A life of righteousness connects the spiritual and material worlds, a heavenly understanding blossoming from faith in the core principle (Christ). Human history is a rich and complex narrative, embroidered with achievements of breathtaking magnitude, extraordinary feats achieved by exceptional individuals—such extraordinary accomplishments, their origin attributed to God's intervention, a divine spark, ignited by a cosmic force, glows with powerful sacred fire.

Within the scriptures, we discover anenduring principle, a methodology demanding reverence and meticulous application:

"One will be blessed and receive the gift who asks, or find the truth who seeks."[24] *(Seeking enlightenment shall bestow God's grace upon the fortunate soul; a fervent quest for knowledge will unveil truths).*

A fundamental reality emerges: Deepest longings instantly materialize within the immaterial world; humanity's destined blessings exist beforehand, immutable gifts woven into God's grand design. Unfold your heart's most fervent desires before Him, invoking the inexhaustible reservoir of infinite abundance and discover an enduring sense of fulfillment. God, wellspring of all bounty understands your most fervent aspirations. However, a sincere eloquent articulation of those yearnings is deeply cherished by the Almighty. Miraculous events of the past powerfully suggest that your future holds equally extraordinary blessings. Embrace this truth and follow the God's guidance that unfolds before you; your needs will be met fully now and for all eternity. Harness the unparalleled power of the sacred Hymns prayer to access an inexhaustible flow of abundance. Deep, consistent communion

---

24. Revelation 1:3

with the infinite source, fueled by resolute faith, will trigger an awakening of divine knowledge and strength, reshaping your very being.

Through the act of recitation, we unlock and amplify the inherent God within, fostering a deep connection to His source. This focused, devotional practice unleashes the hidden power of sacred spirit, elevating it to its fullest expression. *"Be ye transformed yourself by renewing of your mind."*[25] *(Transform yourselves by actively reshape your mental landscape; embrace intellectual rebirth).* To achieve immediate communion with God, you must first, actively dismantle the unconscious barriers that impede your spiritual advancement; this necessitates a shift in deeply held, detrimental beliefs. By cultivating an awareness of your being from head to toe, you will undergo a transformation, evolving into a powerful, dynamic individual brimming with confidence and a comprehension of life's intricate beauty.

---

25. Romans 12:2

Masterful Existence: Fair Play Wins!

Life's resemblance to a game strikes a powerful chord because both encompass inherent structures and unforeseen detours. Just as a game unfolds within complex system of regulations-some overt, others subtly implied -so too does life demand skillful navigation of its intricate framework. These often-unsuspected governing principles mold our journeys, requiring both calculated planning and flexible reactions to unexpected obstacles. The inherent capriciousness and astounding turns of events that characterize existence find their parallel in the unpredictable challenges and thrilling surprises inherent in even the most meticulously designed games, rendering the analogy both moving and revealing.

Triumphing over life's intricate labyrinth requires a grasp of its fundamental mechanisms and governing laws. Proficiently wielding this knowledge, and deploying it with calculated precision, is essential for progress. Importantly, we must foster an unyielding tenacity, adapting our strategies with nimble grace when confronted by unexpected obstacles, thus preserving our resolute course towards our aspirations.

Godsend-celestial messenger declared: *Your inherent, divinely ordained blueprint — a unique tapestry created before your birth — unveils your soul's ultimate purpose; discover your innate, divinely bestowed potential. Unlocking your deepest, most cherished dreams becomes an achievable reality. God's majestic power, a radiant light, guides us along a consecrated, predestined path. It guarantees a voyage untainted by the agony of unmet desires and the bleakness of unproductive striving. Seize your inherent liberty; emancipation is your undeniable legacy.* The scriptures unveil the fundamental truth:

"According to your faith, be it unto you." [26] (*Live your convictions; your faith shall shape your destiny*).

Rapid, resolute action, combined with prayer, dramatically amplifies the power of achieving a deepest desire:

"Tell no one," [27] (*Guard your aspirations wisely; reveal them to none; God's wisdom counsels' secrecy*).

---

26. Matthew 9:29
27. Mark 7:36

"The world belongs to the silent one!"[28] *(The universe favors the discreet).*

Faithful reciting of powerful God's hymns prayer skillfully guides the path to aspiration, actualizing one's destined purpose. Intense concentration on the tangible manifestation of dreams fuels their blossoming. The accuracy of prayer directly reflects the lucidity of the divine response. Uncertainty clouds the journey, breeding vagueness. Resolute commitment to this heavenly practice expedites the achievement of objectives. Persistent, resolute striving hastens the arrival of goals; conversely, apathy can impede advancement, subtly undermining fervent supplications. Time will unveil the genuineness of this longing. A true, God appointed calling burns with fervent zeal, a deep inner conviction inextinguishable and eternally glowing within the soul's core. A deeply ingrained desire, a predetermined path woven into existence, compels our deeds. This intrinsic drive, an undeniable innate vocation, dictates every decision.

---

28. Anonymous

Cultivating a spirit of joy and heartfelt thanksgiving toward Almighty — a reverent acknowledgment of the Alpha and Omega — significantly expedites progress. The fervent devotion forms a powerful bond, a sacred union with the Supreme God.

A powerful bond magnetically draws the life essence, aligning it with your aspirations and ambitions:

"Before ye call I shall answer."[29] *(Prior to your summons, my response will be immediate and decisive).*

Truly, God takes immense pleasure in bestowing upon you these magnificent blessings:

"It is your Father's good pleasure to give you these things."[30] *(Your heavenly Father delights in bestowing these bountiful gifts upon you).*

Understanding that one's deepest desires are fulfilled through deep communion with God's essence reveals a fundamental truth. Sacred prayer, a gift from the heavens, ignites our innate

---

29. Isaiah 65:24
30. Luke 12:32

capabilities, channeling a potent spiritual current. This holy force transmutes our noblest dreams into concrete achievements.

Fulfill Your Destiny

Realizing your highest potential requires a defined path. Unfocused aspiration, devoid of specific goals, squanders its inherent power; this vital energy is wasted, obstructing the realization of any significant achievement. Wasting the exuberant vitality of life breeds a crippling emptiness, a pervasive dissatisfaction that leaves one adrift in a desolate ocean of meaninglessness. Unfulfilled aspirations are a primary source of human misery. Conversely, the attainment of objectives is intrinsically linked to a fulfilling and joyful existence. Therefore, the pursuit and realization of meaningful goals are fundamental to a thriving human life.

With a world brimming with limitless opportunities and seemingly endless assets, discerning which aspirations hold the greatest promise of significant achievement presents a formidable challenge. A dormant power, pregnant with possibility, sleeps within, poised for its explosive emergence and the majestic fulfillment of its intrinsic blueprint. To unearth this ultimate aspiration, carefully chronicle your aspirations, methodically ranking each objective by its inherent worth and potential for personal growth. Lost in a labyrinth of doubt, facing a daunting expanse of potential? Scrutinize your aspirations deeply, exploring the core impulses that fuel every yearning.

Discover the passions that truly set your soul ablaze, aligning with your innermost being. This journey of self-discovery provides insight for those facing uncertain paths. However, the most effective — though not guaranteed — path to identifying your life's purpose lies in seeking spiritual enlightenment. Tap into God's wisdom through fervent prayer and contemplative meditation, allowing heavenly illumination to guide your way.

Often, desires prove illusory, their attainment ultimately detrimental, disappointing, even harmful consequences. Genuine satisfaction, conversely, springs from a steadfast readiness, free from anxiety. Scripture abounds with examples of bravery and fortitude:

"One who is fearless is absolute," (Fearlessness is ultimate self-mastery; courage breeds invincibility)

inner peace arises from conscious and subliminal harmony. Divine Hymns Prayer, a sacred conduit, unlocks the sought-after enlightenment; a celestial illumination brimming with power and spiritual understanding.

Persistent dedication fuels the achievement of ambitions; doubt and apprehension, insidious enemies of noble aspirations, readily warp our intentions if we heed their insidious whispers. These negative forces, initially subtle, quickly escalate into overwhelming and destructive obstacles, jeopardizing our very success. Eradicate the insidious doubts hindering your progress and triumph. Fear, a particularly destructive force, can cripple your aspirations, leading to utter devastation. It's as if fear itself is cruelly distorting your potential, shattering it into irreparable fragments. Conquer this crippling impasse by fostering a resilient divine spirit. Regularly engaging with sacred divine hymns prayer enhances the ability to achieve the goals. Invoke the God's essence, seeking its insightful counsel and a luminous trajectory towards fulfillment. Align your deepest aspirations with your life's true calling, and achievement becomes inevitable. This journey, fueled by fervent passion and intuitive ease, advances with breathtaking speed, yielding swift and profound gratification. Embark on your purposeful quest now, under benevolent guidance, and actualize your magnificent drams.

The Law of Like Attracts Like

The ceaseless God of existence necessitates a vast consumption of vitality; therefore, prudent management of this finite asset is crucial. Wise ancient Greek philosophers, renowned for their insights, discovered a fundamental principle of the universe: homologous energies inherently gravitate toward one another-like attracts like. This universal principle of attraction underscores the inherent spiritual power within each thought—a potent, irresistible force. Its resonance permeates every aspect of our physical and mental existence, powerfully shaping one's existence. Optimism cultivates a fertile ground for success; our inner world shapes external reality, drawing in circumstances that reflect individuals prevailing beliefs, thus nurturing positive achievements. Our feelings generate energetic frequencies that draw similar experiences into our lives. Consequently, cultivating negativity—in mind, speech, and action—engenders an inner conflict, inevitably manifesting as unfortunate consequences since these are the separational emotions with God. Cultivate a genuine desire for love, wealth, and achievement; thoughts will act as a powerful magnet, drawing these aspirations into one's life. In essence, actively shaping one's existence through the powerful force of godly power. Therefore, consider carefully the nature of your requests, for a positive outlook is paramount in forging a fulfilling and purposeful existence.

Success hinges on faith in the harmonious workings of universal spiritual principles. Cultivating an understanding of what constitutes achievement is vital; persistent dedication, fueled by this comprehension is the cornerstone of realizing your aspirations. Sacred writings caution against straying from the ordained path, urging resolute adherence for assured triumph in all endeavors: *"...do not turn from it to the right or to the left, that you may be successful wherever you go."*[31] *(Persistent dedication guarantees ultimate success in every pursuit)*. Obeying God's sacred counsel elevates you to a position of supreme authority, adorned with the glorious crown of integrity. This divine decree further mandates unwavering commitment: *"...meditate on it day and night, so that you may be careful to do everything written in it. Then you will be*

---

31. Joshua 1: 7

prosperous and successful."[32] (*Let your purpose be etched upon your heart, a constant meditation, day and night. Diligent adherence to its sacred precepts guarantees a life of flourishing abundance and triumph*). Complementing this fundamental principle, cultivating stillness amplifies inherent God's power.

Throughout history, spiritual seekers have embraced the sanctuary of silence; this refuge safeguards aspirations from disruptive forces. It preserves the soul's pristine essence, allowing inner illumination to blossom and radiate outwards.

---

32. Joshua 1: 8

Break the Cycle of Misery

A subtle, creeping cynicism, a malignant viper of hopelessness, relentlessly constricts our ambitions, suffocating the tender growth of our belief and determination. While the divine hand of God tirelessly labors for our ultimate good, a malignant force relentlessly strives to undermine God's children, corrupting every facet of our existence. This relentless assault seeks to shatter our resolve and thwart the fulfillment of God's plan. Giving credence to the subtle whispers of despair, only amplifies their corrosive power. This self-defeating cycle intensifies, culminating in devastating consequences. The Scripture echo this heavenly truth:

"The heart is deceitful above all things, and desperately sick; who can understand it?" [33] *(The human heart is treacherous, a vessel of incurable malady. Its depths are inscrutable; who can truly fathom its complexities and maintain a grasp on its elusive nature?).*

---

33. Jeremiah 17:9

"The thief comes only to steal and kill and destroy."[34] *(The adversary-Satan, seeks the complete annihilation of all virtue).* The enemy aims to utterly destroy all that is good; yet, positive outlook, a structured mental process mirroring its negative counterpart, yields to the transformational power of the Divine. Heartfelt prayer will be answered:

"…Whatever you ask in prayer, you will receive, if you have faith."[35] *(Faithful supplication yields abundant blessings).*

"For nothing will be impossible with God."[36] *(God's omnipotence transcends limitations, rendering all things attainable).*

Harmful ideologies gain ascendancy due to a neglect of our positive convictions. This crucial truth underscored in the Scripture. *"Do not be overcome by evil, but overcome evil with good."*[37] *(Overcome evil with goodness-Conquer malevolence not by succumbing to its darkness, but by vanquishing it with the radiant power of virtue).* This underscores

---

34. John 10:10
35. Matthew 21:22
36. Luke 1:37
37. Romans 12:21

the critical importance of diligently fostering and fiercely defending virtuous principles.

Remember this essential wisdom: God's judgment is immutable and absolute; the consequences of one's actions are inescapable:

"Do not be deceived: God is not mocked, for whatever one sows, that will he also reap."[38] *(Beware of illusion: God's justice is resolute. The consequences of one's actions are inescapable; every deed yields its inevitable harvest).* Holy texts reveal a rich spiritual treasure:

"But the fruit of the divine Spirit is love, joy, peace, patience, kindness, goodness, faithfulness;"[39] *(The essence of a Godly inspired life blossom into affection, elation, serenity, forbearance, benevolence, virtue, and unwavering loyalty).* These breathtaking displays reveal ever-present love of God.

These breathtaking displays reveal an ever-present love of God. Unchain yourself from the prison of despair and begin a transformatory odyssey toward complete physical and spiritual renewal:

---

38. Galatians 6:7
39. Galatians 5:22

"Whatever is true, whatever is honorable, whatever is just, whatever is pure, whatever is lovely, whatever is commendable, if there is any excellence, if there is anything worthy of praise, think about these things."[40] *(Focus your mind on virtues: truth's radiant light, noble actions, righteous conduct, unsullied purity, exquisite beauty, praiseworthy deeds. Let your thoughts dwell on all that is excellent, all that merits the highest acclaim).*

Our anxieties flourish on the attention we lavish upon them; withdrawing that investment weakens their hold. Complex, self-sustaining predicaments often succumb not to forceful scrutiny, but to the quiet grace of mindful, receptive contemplation. Surrender anxieties, and tranquility blossoms; their ability to wound or distress vanishes. This transformative change unveils radically new viewpoints, reshaping our perception of existence in a breathtaking way. Life's trajectory originates in the depths of our inner being. Sacred texts powerfully emphasize this truth:

"Above all else, guard your heart, for everything you do flows from it."[41] *(Prioritize the protection*

---

40. Philippians 4:8
41. Proverbs 4:6

of your soul; all your actions and choices spring from its core).

Embrace an abundance mentality; actively dismantle the crippling belief that life is inherently arduous and fraught with disappointment. The agony of lingering resentment demands unwavering fortitude, as its corrosive influence poisons mind, body, and spirit, permeating every facet of your being. Fixating on past spiritual encounters fosters a paralyzing inertia, a mental stagnation. Valuable chances for growth and advancement vanish, unrealized, as you remain shackled to the ghosts of yesterday, instead of seizing the present's immense capacity for transformation. Dwelling on past grievances and excessive chatter dissipate your inherent strength. Early influences instilled detrimental habits, effectively shackling your potential and preventing you from realizing life's abundant rewards. This crucial moment demands unwavering concentration: pierce the veil of illness, revealing inherent well-being; transcend constraints, and embrace overflowing prosperity. Sacred writings assure us:

"The Lord will grant you abundant prosperity...."[42]
(Divine favor will shower you with overflowing wealth and boundless success).

Daily invocation of sacred hymns prayers unlocks God's potential, hastening the arrival of celestial blessings. This practice mends the devastation of past misfortunes, restoring lost years of prosperity and abundance, or even forging a wholly new life brimming with divine wealth. Harnessing the potent energy of its sacred core, you'll undergo a transformative quantum leap, your inherent divinity revitalized and superseded by an empowering influx of celestial might and triumphant destiny. Your transformed existence will become strikingly evident to those around you, revealing a distinct and powerful shift in your leadership and existence.

---

42. Deuteronomy 28:11

The Holy Ark: Divine Revelation

Deep within resides an innate brilliance, dormant yet attainable. Cultivating a receptive spirit unlocks this latent genius. Unlock your potential:

"Awake thou that sleepeth."[43] *(Arise, slumbering soul, and embrace this path of potential).*

Inner guidance of divine wisdom, yields deeper understanding and exceptional achievement—humanity's greatest discovery. History's most influential figures ascended to greatness by harnessing this inherent wisdom, their perceptive insights propelling them to unparalleled leadership. The God's perception provides an expeditious path to discerning the core truth of any situation. Da Vinci's genius illuminated the pivotal role of sensory perception in the genesis of understanding. Our comprehension, he asserted, *"All our knowledge has its origin in our perceptions;"* springs entirely from what we perceive, thus opening a pathway to limitless potential and flourishing. From the

---

43. Ephesians 5:14

depths of the unconscious, a brilliant revelation erupts, a momentary flash of understanding, a powerful premonition, or a compelling inner voice. A breathtaking discovery, urgently demanding attention, illuminates the route to previously concealed treasure. Hidden fortunes, slyly disguised as insignificant details, whisper their secrets through destiny's capricious hand. What initially appears inconsequential can dramatically reveal the crux of the matter, casting a brilliant light upon the path to one's most cherished goal. A celestial design, surpassing intricate confusion, unveils a breathtaking, long-yearned-for prize with astonishing suddenness.

Vision, a divine and potent sensory tool, unlocks countless mysteries. Our desires materialize through its perceptive power; true omniscience stems from mastering the art of seeing and many examples are written in the Scripture. Enduring myths starkly illuminate humanity's naiveté concerning cosmic origins, a universe frustratingly elusive to our comprehension. Lacking insightful revelation, our cosmological knowledge remains tragically circumscribed. Timeless cultural insights, subtly unveiled through layered scriptural interpretations. A failure to perceive life's nuanced tapestry reveals a stark disconnect from the universe's intricate web:

"When man loses his sight, he loses his view of the universe."[44] *(Blindness diminishes a person's perception of the cosmos, severing their connection to the vast expanse of existence; without internal clarity, global understanding crumbles).* Our eyes serve as the essential portal through which the soul's deepest wisdom is revealed.

Possessing unparalleled intellect, Godly favored King Solomon made a momentous declaration: A life surrendered to God guidance blossoms into a cornucopia of prosperity, prestige, robust health, and unyielding joy. Sacred scripture attests to this enduring verity:

"Trust in the Lord with all your heart and lean not on your own understanding (intellect); in all your ways submit to him, and he will make your paths straight."[45] *(Trust God completely, abandoning self-reliance. Humble obedience to His will, will enlighten your path.).*

---

44. Anonymous
45. Proverbs 3:5-6

We have all experienced moments Stunning revelation, flashing moments of truth, breathtaking in their luminous revelation leave us speechless. These pivotal moments renew the enduring bond:

"Commit your way to the Lord; trust in him and he will make your righteous reward...."[46] *(Surrender your path to God's guidance; place your absolute faith in Him and He will bestow upon you a divinely just recompense).*

To access the boundless potential, childlike innocence is the essential key, as holy texts reveal. Remain resolutely committed to your predestined path; unwavering faith guarantees an abundant and glorious recompense.

---

46. Psalm 37:5-6

Hopes and Dreams

Sacred texts eloquently portray hope and aspirations, inextricably linked to God's purpose and covenants. While worldly expectations may falter or shatter, faith-based hope stands unshaken, a wellspring of joy. God's intentions for the faithful are inherently benevolent, promising a future brimming with optimism and assurance:

"For I know the plans I have for you," declares the Lord, "Plans to prosper you and not to harm you, plans to give you hope and a future." [47] *(God's plan for you is a life of prosperity, not hardship; a future radiant with hope and joy, leading to a blessed destiny. He desires your success and happiness)*. This scripture forms the bedrock of God's commitment to sustain and enrich the lives of His devoted followers. This implies God's capacity and willingness to grant the heartfelt petitions of the faithful:

"But those who hope in the Lord will renew their strength. They will soar on wings like eagles; they will run and not grow weary, they will walk

---

47. Jeremiah 29:11

and not be faint."[48] *(God's faithful will find renewed strength. They will rise like eagles, soaring effortlessly, their commitment carrying them far).*

"Hope deferred makes the heart sick, but a dream fulfilled is a tree of life."[49] *(Unfulfilled longing breeds despair, while the realization of a cherished aspiration yields joy and enduring vitality).* This passage recognizes the agonizing sting of adversity. Faith in God, however ultimately yields contentment and enduring happiness.

"Delight yourself in the Lord, and he will give you the desires of your heart."[50] *(Find your joy in the Lord, and He will abundantly fulfill your heart's deepest longings).*

"May he give you the desire of your heart and make all your plans succeed."[51] *(May your deepest aspirations blossom into reality, and may every endeavor you undertake be crowned with resounding success).*

"May the God of hope fill you with all joy and peace as you trust in him, so that you may

---

48. Isaiah 40:31
49. Proverbs 13:12
50. Psalm 37:4
51. Psalm 20:4

overflow with hope by the power of the Holy Spirit."[52] *(Trust in the Almighty, and let Him fill you with joy and peace. This faith, empowered by the Holy Spirit, will make you a beacon of eternal hope, radiating blessings).*

"Seek first the Kingdon of God and His righteousness and all these things will be added to you."[53] *(Prioritize God's reign and moral uprightness above all else, and you will find that everything necessary will be abundantly provided).*

This passage champions a life rooted in faith and reliance upon God's providence, powerfully assuring devotees that their needs will be met when they prioritize seeking God's guidance. Genuine contentment stems not from fleeting earthly riches or transient worldly ambitions, but from an enduring connection with the Divine.

Scripture reveals the pathway to fulfilling the aspirations. Instead of years spent adrift in uncertainty, a clear, efficient route is illuminated. Our earthly pursuits — the relentless chase of hopes and dreams — are inextricably

---

52. Romans 15:13
53. Matthew 6:33

interwoven with God's world. Those attuned to the spiritual dimension perceive this deep connection, recognizing our secular existence as greatly dependent on God's grace, the source of all blessings. This sacred truth, unveiled by God himself within the Scriptures, offers a transformative understanding of life's journey.

Before the Almighty, bow in humble supplication, seeking His benevolent grace. Yield one's desires to the Creator's infinite majesty, aligning with God's flow. With devotion, journey along the consecrated path He has ordained. Let God's hymns echo in your heart, a silent conversation that fills you with glorious, ethereal energy. Nurture your deepest aspirations, tending them within the sacred chambers of your heart until their glorious blossoming. Cultivate a spirit attuned solely to the holy, a vessel receptive only to God. Begin by inviting God's presence, petitioning the Holy Spirit's sanctifying power. Simultaneously, raise a strong spiritual shield around your spirit, resisting protective verses before the sacred work. Filling your thoughts with noble aims and yearnings; these are holy seeds, planted in your soul's rich earth, destined to yield abundant blessings, their influence resonating throughout the infinite Divine.

Culminating in a majestic declaration—"So ordained, gratitude ascends"—the revered Golden Hymns achieve their zenith. This sacred vow, a celestial pact, reverberates with intensified power, solidifying the divine design. Mirroring the initial invocation, this concluding affirmation gracefully frames the entire ritual, crafting a narrative of breathtaking resonance and impact. A boundless, God's fountainhead pours forth unending blessings, a heavenly torrent of grace. This final prayer stands as an invincible shield, deflecting malevolence and guaranteeing the fulfillment of your deepest desires – the very foundation of this sacred covenant. This potent invocation forms a conduit, linking your yearning for cosmic harmony to the divine source itself.

Now, at this critical crossroads, Let the divinely, echoing chants of the hymns commence. Their God's tones in this pivotal moment ignites the inexorable march in your predetermined destiny. Each day, choose divine hymns that stir your soul's depth. Through devout supplication, form an unshakable connection with God, hastening the arrival of your heart's truest aspirations. Through consecrated devotion and dedication, this solemn agreement signifies a hard-won triumph.

With faith, prepare for miracles that will leave you breathless. God's magnificent, inventive power will dramatically reshape one's existence. A spiritual bond with the God exponentially increases the expectation with Him, accelerating the unveiling of extraordinary blessings with irresistible momentum. Undertake this life-altering pilgrimage, a voyage into the depths of your soul, fostering spiritual awakening.

Live a Miraculous Life

A conviction firmly rooted in one's core being fuels a philosophy of nonresistance; Their unshakeable faith in the core principle demands a completely indispensable strategy:

"Don't choose but follow an inspiration."[54] *(Allow your inspiration to direct you; eschew deliberate selection).*

Divine inspiration, a source of inner knowing, provides unparalleled access to universal concord. Blind adherence to Aristotelian logic obstructs the transcendent flow of God's insight. This inflexible methodology, it seems, masks a distrust of spiritually revealed knowledge. Inspiration and reason appear to be fundamentally incompatible bedfellows in the realm of pure intellect, existing in a state of dissonance. Creative genius, a fragile, incandescent flame, often vanishes under the cold, relentless scrutiny of logic; these opposing forces, potent and mutually destructive, clash like thunder and lightning. Following God's direction prevents the crushing weight of

---

54. Anonymous

regrettable decisions and disastrous courses of action. Embracing celestial guidance grants a sanctuary of strength and assistance, shielding one from the bitter consequences of innocent folly. Spiritual awakening provides an immeasurable and profound benefit.

Prayer: Conversation with God

Prayer, once a sacred ritual, has sadly declined, becoming a forgotten vestige of a bygone era. Consumed by the relentless tide of modern life, we squander precious moments, neglecting communion with the Almighty until the final reckoning. Our souls, starved for spiritual sustenance, remain adrift in a sea of worldly concerns, postponing connection with God's until it's too late. We readily embrace both God's intervention and medical expertise in moments of suffering, yet these pillars of support are often abandoned as soon as the storm subsides. The intensity of prayer and the desperate search for medical solutions are inversely proportional to the receding threat. Once the peril diminishes, so too does our commitment to the higher powers and learned professionals who guided us through the ordeal. Sinner peace isn't a temporary balm for life's wounds; it's an enduring necessity, a fundamental truth to be integrated into the very core of our being. Let devotion serve as a powerful preventative, a steadfast shield against the inevitable storms of life. Humanity's deepest longing, as Plutarch eloquently portrays:

"The hearts and souls of men still seek the Deity and desire the experience of the God."[55] *(Humanity's deepest yearnings persistently gravitate toward the Divine, craving an intimate communion with God).*

For ages, sacred texts and revered spiritual guides have powerfully affirmed prayer's transformative influence, presenting it as a potent conduit to the divine realm. At its core, prayer constitutes a consecrated dialogue with the Supreme Being, a conscious act of worship fostering a deep, reciprocal bond. A vibrant, engaged spiritual community nurtures this vital connection to the transcendent, strengthening the reciprocal relationship between humanity and God. Genuine, efficacious prayer hinges upon confidence in God's limitless power. The fervent blaze of faith ignites our entreaties; without it, they become empty rituals, adrift in a sea of insignificance, failing to pierce the veil of the unseen. Prayer's immense capacity resides in its ability to alter our very being—physically, mentally, and spiritually. Through steadfast faith, communion with the Creator sparks remarkable,

---

55. Plutarch: A philosophical letter of consolation, (Moralia) Vol. II pp. 105

life-altering events, leading to epiphanies that reshape individual's existence.

Prayer, deeply rooted in scripture and theological doctrines, constitutes the cornerstone of humanity's spiritual ascent, a practice as ancient as civilization itself. Its timeless influence reverberates with an almost incomprehensible power, shaping the course of human experience in lasting ways. Humanity's innate spiritual longing draws upon an infinite wellspring of insight, compassion, and valor—a limitless ocean of intellectual enlightenment.

Throughout history, the lives of devout individuals bear witness to this search, their passionate prayers echoing a relentless pursuit of absolute truth. Through devotion to divine practices, they achieved enlightenment, their existence illuminated by a brilliance born of exceptional wisdom. Through contemplative-prayer practice, the breathtaking grandeur of nature surpassed simple beauty. It manifested as a radiant, boundless paradigm—a majestic pinnacle embodying unwavering fortitude, intrinsic power and an indomitable spirit. Humility, piety, kindness and empathy defined these spiritually awakened individuals. Their quest for enlightenment transcended rigid dogma; they yearned for the unblemished, indivisible core of God—a pristine, celestial essence. These noble qualities formed the bedrock of their extraordinary existence.

Fundamentally, through prayer, we form a sacred relationship with the divine, a conscious offering of reverence fostering a vibrant, mutually enriching bond with God—a dynamic, deeply personal spiritual embrace. The genuine power of prayer depends entirely upon unshakeable faith in the God Almighty's boundless capacity; otherwise, our petitions become empty gestures, a fruitless expedition lost at sea, forever failing to reach their destined haven. Prayer's fundamental power lies in its capacity to alter our lives, impacting our physical well-being, mental clarity, and spiritual growth. Resolute faith illuminates the way ahead, forming a connection with the sacred that triggers transformative, epochal occurrences. These revelations dramatically altered the trajectory of countless lives.

To communion with the God demands utmost humility. Thus, to access God's limitless mercy, cultivate a spiritual intimacy. This sacred merging demands meticulous preparation, a vital precursor to unveiling your soul's deepest yearnings. Discover the incandescent core of being—that passionate aspiration, life's purpose, the very bedrock of your existence. Before intoning the revered Golden Hymns, nurture a serene, contemplative quietude. This meditative stillness, paramount to the efficacy of supplication, aligns with God, ensuring your desires resonate with celestial power. Be ready; this alignment amplifies the potency of the prayer. As this preparatory ritual becomes second nature, a vibrant, palpable energy will thrum within, a testament to the sacred connection has established. Sacred texts offer an illustration of the process of divine communication:

"Then you will call on me and come and pray to me and I will listen to you. You will seek me and find me when you seek me with all your heart." [56] (*Seek me earnestly in prayer, and I will hear your pleas. Only fervent devotion reveals me*).

"Be anxious for nothing, but in everything by prayer and petition, with thanksgiving, let your

---

56. Jeremiah 29:12-13

requests be made known to God; and the peace of God which surpasses all understanding, will guard your hearts and minds through Christ Jesus."[57] (Release all worry. Pour out your heart to God in prayer, giving thanks and voicing your deepest needs, trusting Him completely. Then receive God's surpassing peace, a tranquility beyond comprehension, as your comfort. Through Christ, I will protect your heart and mind).

"Therefore, confess your sins to each other and pray for each other so that you may be healed the prayer of a righteous person is powerful and effective."[58] (Confess flaws to each other and sincerely advocate for one another. Embrace mutual vulnerability and heartfelt prayer. Honest supplication holds power; it can restore wholeness).

Seek a serene interlude, a sanctuary of stillness. Center yourself, and with ceaseless devotion, call upon the God, inviting the incandescent radiance of the Divine. Deep, resonant breaths, repeated many times, will amplify your connection. Visualize the presence of God, a luminous embrace that suffuses your being with its sacred light.

---

57. Philippians 4:6-7
58. James 5:16

Faith: Secret of Manifestation

History unveils a stunning truth: a belief in the divine underpins the intellectual giants who have molded our civilization, transcending the boundaries of their respective fields. Consider Pythagoras, a towering figure of ancient Greece whose groundbreaking contributions to mathematics and philosophy stemmed from an intense, personal communion with the sacred. His contemplation of existence's ultimate nature revealed a ubiquitous divinity, its very being synonymous with ultimate reality. Similarly, sacred scriptures echo with a wisdom of unparalleled profundity, resonating across millennia:

"Infinite Being, whose body was composed of the substance of truth."[59] (*The boundless, divine essence forms the eternal heart of existence*).

A human longing, recognized by philosophical giants like Plato and Socrates, is the inherent desire to worship a supreme, all-encompassing power, or the ancient deities believed to spring from the source of existence. Prayer, a vital thread in the

---

59. Betegh, Gabor, Pythagoreans, Orphism and Greek Religion, in Huffman 2014a,.149-157

human tapestry, intensely magnifies our most heartfelt ambitions. This inherent capacity lifts our cherished aspirations to a celestial realm. Through the confluence of supplication and divine direction, we commence a journey of self-discovery. This process reveals our intrinsic purpose within the cosmos, enabling us to undergo a life-altering metamorphosis.

Fervent desire awakens God's essence, a humble plea for grace to saturate our ambitions and shower us with boundless blessings. Submersion in the Holy Trinity unleashes extraordinary wonders, catalyzing metamorphosis across body, mind and spirit—a momentous stride toward God's grand vision for humankind. Prayer, irrespective of creed or its significance, acts as a sacred route to God, a universally available pathway to the transcendent, enriching every aspect of our lives.

The principle of God's right emphasizes prayer's crucial role in all aspects of human existence: personal, collective and societal. Sacred texts echo this essential truth, urging us to infuse our lives with persistent prayer and heartfelt thanksgiving. The scripture reveals:

"Make your life a prayer. And in the midst of everything be always giving thanks, for this is God's perfect plan for you in Christ."[60] *(Live a life of resolute faith. Embrace gratitude amidst life's challenges; this is God's plan, guided by Christ's love).*

Embracing this reality attracts God's blessings. Consistent spiritual discipline—prayer, entreaty, heartfelt worship—catalyzes a phenomenal metamorphosis. The boundless mercy of God empowers those who earnestly pursue it, nurturing a personal evolution. The Scriptures reveal truths:

"...Whatever you ask in prayer, you will receive, if you have faith.";[61] *(Request anything through earnest prayer: ask, and you shall receive; believe, and it will be yours-Faithful supplication, filled with faith, unlocks the door to your heart's desires).*

"...Whatever you ask in prayer, believe that you have received it, and it will be yours."[62] *With unwavering faith, petition God; possess the unshakeable conviction that your supplication is already granted, and its fulfillment shall be yours).* God's benevolent

---

60. 1 Thessalonians 5:17
61. Matthew 21:22
62. Mark 11:22

hand guides every prayer, embracing our whole being—body, mind, spirit, and the ancestral legacy bequeathed to us.

The legacy of ancestral pain, a cruel inheritance of bitterness and spite, casts an inescapable shadow of torment, defying all attempts at redemption. Generational trauma, a grim inheritance, perpetuates cycles of anguish impervious to conventional healing. Only a miraculous intervention from the Almighty can shatter these bonds, purify the spirit and bestow tranquility. This liberation arises from sincere contrition and fervent supplication. The promise is absolute: even the most entrenched, multi-generational afflictions yield to the power of a believing heart. The eminent theologian Augustine illuminated the connection between prayer and desire, declaring, *"Prayer is the desire of the soul."*[63] *(From the core of our longing, fervent pleas ascend).* All divine grace flows from the hand of the Almighty. The sincerity of a prayer, whether a passionate plea or a humble reflection, determines its worth; its efficacy

---

63. Augustine, From discourse on the Psalms, Psalm 37, 13-14, pp.391-392

rests solely on the depth of devotion within the supplicant's heart.

To those who understand prayer's immense power, its ability to summon God's intervention is undeniable. Passed down through millennia, the capacity of this practice to foster holistic well-being—a harmonious blend of mental acuity, physical vitality and spiritual enlightenment—has remained an enduring and immutable principle. In stark contrast to today's sophisticated medical interventions, pre-modern populations endured excruciating agony, bereft of both scientific understanding and the tools of surgical alleviation. Humanity's innate suffering, inherited from our earliest beginnings, is a relentless, daily burden. Each person desperately seeks respite from this pervasive affliction, longing for enduring peace and happiness. The crushing weight of illness and disease, a constant shadow throughout life, forms a crucial element of this perpetual struggle, its prevalence a grim record stretching back to the earliest writings.

Paracelsus, the groundbreaking fifteenth-century physician, a visionary ahead of his time boldly posited a connection between widespread psychological anguish—anxiety and stress—and the etiology of numerous physical ailments. This insightful assertion, once considered radical, finds compelling corroboration in contemporary medical understanding. His insightful wisdom, remarkably prescient, rested on a timeless truth: human affliction often originates from a toxic concoction of bitterness, fear, jealousy, and ill will simmering within the human spirit. He proposed a principle: the majority of diseases take root in the obscure depths of the subliminal mind – a tangled web of thoughts and memories – only later manifesting as excruciating physical suffering.

Paracelsus's insightful wisdom reveals a powerful, omnipresent spiritual force mirroring and amplifying the core beliefs and personal truths residing within our souls. Involuntary or deliberate, these ingrained mental images inevitably materialize as concrete, physical existence. Paracelsus asserted that fervent supplications—sacred prayers, heartfelt prayers, and solemn statements—constitute powerful declarations of conviction, intrinsically interwoven with faith. This vibrant belief serves as a formidable catalyst for quantum realization, a dynamic energy propelling the manifestation of cherished desires and yearnings. Devout prayer transcends the mundane, lifting the spirit and imbuing the soul with righteous emotion and the unwavering certainty of God's ultimate restorative power.

The confluence of human consciousness and God's grace triggers a biological and spiritual transformation. Genuine faith unleashes the innate, restorative power of the sacred, exponentially hastening the journey of self-transformation. An everlasting devotion, even amidst seemingly insurmountable challenges, necessitates a complete surrender to the awesome power of the Almighty. The Scripture counsels us to seek the guidance of the enlightened, wisdom will undeniably follow. Conversely, association with the unthinking invites calamitous consequences. Wickedness invariably attracts devastating retribution, while virtuous conduct reaps abundant rewards. As the Proverb wisely states:

"Walk with the wise and become wise, for a companion of fools suffers harm. Trouble pursues the sinner, but the righteous are rewarded with

good things"[64] *(Close association with the wise makes one wise; friendship with fools brings ruin. Misfortune relentlessly pursues the wicked, but blessings crown the lives of the righteous).*

Paracelsus posited that the fundamental blueprints of our existence, our most yearnings, are an immutable fate, orchestrated by God's hand, is shaped by the inextricable intertwining of ancestral legacy and innate proclivities. God's grace and faith ignite an innate capacity for creation. However, even the most encompassing shadows succumb to the potent, redemptive power of authentic faith. Faith, he proclaimed, was the sole, infallible cure; prayer devoid of such steadfast conviction degenerated into hollow formality. Genuine faith transcends mere acceptance; it's a trust, a holy pact uniting humankind with God's power pervading the universe. This bond establishes a sacred architecture—a realm of unwavering conviction, a spiritual fountainhead pulsing with vital energy. Across diverse societies, a legacy of spiritual healing persists. Powerful invocations, sacred chants, impassioned pleas, and resolute declarations are employed to revitalize

---

64. Proverbs 13:20-21

the physical form and harmonize its ethereal energy systems, achieving a state of balance. Genuine, unwavering belief in recovery produces demonstrable results. In contrast, a stubborn adherence to the misconception of inescapable or fated sickness renders even the most fervent pleas ineffectual, a futile ritual of entreaty.

Urgent Plea: Unleash God's Gift

The Scripture illustrate that persistent prayer ultimately triumphs over fervent desire:

"Even if an evil judge could be worn down by being asked over and over for help, God will also hear the prayers of his people who pray day and night."[65] *(Even the most resolute foe yields to persistent prayer. God's power overwhelms all opposition; a watchful protector heeds the faithful's fervent pleas.).*

While God's all-knowing nature fully comprehends the deepest longings of the soul, passionate supplications most authentically reflect His wisdom. A personal connection with the Almighty is not merely a pious act, but a vibrant, powerful expression of faith. Such earnest pleas resonate deeply within God's infinite compassion, a sublime manifestation of ceaseless devotion. History reveals a compelling correlation: individuals intensely committed to spiritual practices and an intimate communion with the sacred have often experienced phenomenal occurrences that elude rational comprehension.

---

65. Luke 18:7

Miraculous events seem inextricably bound to the passionate recitation of sacred hymns delivered by a Godsent. These hymns, a resonant from countless appellations of the God Almighty, possess an inherent power that catalyzes these extraordinary occurrences. The Scriptures unveil a timeless wisdom. Persistent supplication unlocks the universe's bounty:

"Ask and it will be given to you; seek and you will find; knock and the door will be opened to you. For everyone who asks receives; the one who seeks finds; and to the one who knocks, the door will be opened."[66] *(Request, and you shall receive; search, and you shall discover; knock, and the door will open. Persistence yields reward- Fierce dedication unveils deep fulfillment; ardent longing unlocks your heart's deepest desires).*

The dedication to prayer, the relentless chase of a dream, the passionate plea for breakthrough — these actions invariably yield their bounty. Yet, many scoff, dismissing this age-old wisdom as a childish fantasy, a mere concoction of hope. This pervasive disbelief arises from a grim, societal

---

66. Matthew 7:7-8

conditioning—a pervasive cynicism deeply etched into our collective psyche. We're taught, from cradle to grave, that life is an unrelenting battle, a Sisyphean struggle against insurmountable odds. Comfort, we are told, is a mirage; success, a hard-won prize extracted through agonizing toil. This pervasive pessimism, this suffocating sense of inevitable adversity, casts a long shadow over our aspirations.

God's benevolent plan ensures that passionate supplication reaps abundant rewards. Yet, humanity's capacity for spiritual connection remains tragically underdeveloped, a vast reservoir of potential unrealized. The chief obstacle, it appears, stems from a misapprehension of the correct approach to divine communion. The Scripture issue an urgent plea:

Master, instruct us in the art of supplication: *"Lord, teach us to pray."*[67] (God Almighty, grant us the gift of heartfelt prayer).

This journey surpasses mere formality—the physical mechanics, environmental context, or temporal constraints are inconsequential. It is

---

67. Luke 11:1

a deeply personal, spiritual striving, essential groundwork for sacred union. This transformative process fosters an unquenchable thirst for the divine presence, a yearning that springs from the soul's very depths. For the heart, as scripture reveals, is the fountainhead of all existence, the authentic core of our identity:

from it (the heart) flow the springs of life."[68] *(From the heart's deepest chambers surge the life force, a torrent of vibrant energy).*

"The Lord is near to all who call on him, to all who call on him in truth."[69] *(God is readily accessible to those who earnestly seek him, to every soul that invokes his name with genuine devotion).*

Connection with God is a priceless, inherent human capacity, a sacred birthright shared by all. This unparalleled access to the transcendent realm through prayer is an immeasurable blessing. Yet, for many, true intimacy with God—a mystical union with the ultimate reality—remains a challenging aspiration. This hallowed portal, leading to God's boundless grace, constitutes the

---

68. Proverbs 4:23
69. Psalm 145:18

very core of the spiritual quest; it's a precious gift from the Creator, a summons extended only to those deemed receptive to its enigmas:

"One who becomes the master of faith, also becomes the master in every aspect of life."[70] (*Achieving ultimate spiritual enlightenment grants unparalleled dominion over every aspect of being*).

The supplicant who prays with faith and humble acceptance, their petition imbued with unshakeable trust, will find their pleas answered. For faith, the bedrock of the divine covenant, assures:

"Trust in me (faith) and I will bring it to pass."[71] (*Entrust yourself to me, and I shall fulfill your desires*).

Faith forms the bedrock of manifestation; it's the indispensable engine driving personal metamorphosis.

---

70. Pope John Paul II, Congregation for the Doctrine of the Faith, V. 24, p.8 1990
71. Psalm 37:5

PART III

God's Intervention: Miraculous Manifestation

"Blessed are those who find wisdom, those who gain understanding,..." [1]

(Fortunate are the insightful, those who diligently embrace sagacity, those who grasp truths and allow such wisdom to shape their lives).

---

1. Proverbs 3:13

GOLDEN BOUGH: Concealed Divine Wisdom

The mysteries of the Almighty, the Supreme Being and decipher the rich, symbolic language inherent in certain colors. Jewish tradition richly illuminates the significance of gold and red in their connection to the Almighty, as detailed in the Torah, Talmud, Kabbalah, Midrash, and rabbinic writings. Gold, reigning supreme, dominates the description of the Tabernacle in Exodus. Kabbalistic interpretation elevates this golden majesty, viewing it as a representation of divine judgment—yet a judgment characterized by mercy and refinement. The meticulous craftsmanship, with gold hammered exceedingly thin and interwoven with other vibrant threads, powerfully symbolizes judgment's pervasive presence throughout creation, not as a detached, brutal power, but as an integral, nuanced aspect of existence. Moreover, the symbolism of gold deepens, interwoven with the Kabbalistic Sefirot—God attributes—and their inherent characteristics.

The Talmud's crimson hue intensifies the potent link to bloodshed and transgression. Within

Kabbalistic lore, this chromatic resonance signifies *gevurah*—the formidable force of judgment and discipline—potentially embodying a shadow side of spiritual power. Gold transcends mere embellishment; it embodies God's sanctifying grace, a potent force capable of healing and liberating us from the burdens that afflict our bodies, minds, and souls. Reserved solely for God, this luminous hue surpasses earthly constraints, blazing as an incandescent emblem of enlightenment, unparalleled sagacity, and the assurance of immortality. It showers us with resplendent mercy, protection, support and an inviolable bulwark against malevolent influences. This inner luminescence, a force of unparalleled might, obliterates all that deviates from God's plan. It utterly dismantles manifestations of hardship—illness, poverty, want—neutralizing any threat to well-being, any weapon aimed at inflicting physical damage. Several passages from sacred scripture powerfully illustrate this point. These selected verses, among countless others, offer insights and compelling evidence. Their eloquent messages resonate deeply, providing significant support for the central theme.

The ancient wisdom embedded in the Golden Hymns reveals a powerful, illuminating essence—a vibrant pathway to spiritual awakening. These sacred invocations provide solace and strength, shielding the heart from life's relentless onslaughts on physical, mental, and emotional well-being, thus fostering remarkable personal transformation. Breaking free from the insidious weight of inherited trauma, they rise above the suffocating legacy of ancestral despair. A celestial surge of power, piercing the subconscious mind's darkest depths, kindles a transformative blaze. This purifying fire consumes inherited darkness, revealing the inherent splendor of the soul, a radiant self-reborn. This method serves as a powerful comfort, renewing the depleted essence at both conscious and unconscious levels, thus guiding the individual toward holistic and fulfilling well-being.

The sacred act of reciting holy verses, a divine gift, ignites a potent flow of spiritual power, forming a great link between the soul and its ultimate source. A surge of cosmic energy, amplified to unimaginable levels, triggers a quantum flow. This powerful wave washes away inherited suffering and past wounds, a cleansing tide of grace that leaves the spirit reborn, renewed, and liberated. The inherited wounds of the past, the insidious blight of despair and defeat, the deep-seated psychic injuries—these ancestral curses are at last vanquished, resulting in a soul reborn, purified and whole. Spiritual renewal brings peace, flooding the spirit with exuberant gladness and revitalized being. The oppressive burden of past injustices dissolves, ushering in an era of emancipation and optimism; hope blossoms anew.

This consecrated hymn, a conduit of spiritual energy, delivers only the purest grace of the God, the inherent gift uplifting and inspired, acts solely to enhance and strengthen. Its core is completely free from ill will or antagonism; its purpose is purely beneficial. Our spiritual journey requires a lexicon that mirrors our highest ideals. It is crucial to abandon language redolent with hopelessness, such as "malevolent destiny," "a life of unrelenting hardship," "inadequate being," or "a cursed inheritance"—terms that suffocate the spirit with negativity and self-reproach. The insidious insertion of such phrasing within the sacred hymns prayer threatens to implant destructive, self-limiting beliefs deep within the psyche, thereby risking the transmission of a legacy of despair across countless generations. Fill your vocabulary with words radiating optimism, resolute faith, and spiritual growth, nurturing a rich, affirmative inner landscape. Let your language become a beacon of hope, deliberately constructing a life that reflects your greatest aspirations.

Invoking God's Presence

The core of supplication lies in the earnest plea directed toward God of Most High seeking comfort, intervention or enlightenment. Calling upon God requires heartfelt prayer, a spirit of humility and the respectful utterance of God's sacred name. A longing for God's presence, guidance and tangible manifestations of the sacred permeates daily life within the Judeo-Christian tradition, deeply ingrained in its cultural fabric. The Old Testament resounds with the fervent pleas of pious souls, their earnest invocations, the divine reflecting a conviction in God's boundless power and ever-present nearness. This practice established a sacred tradition, their devotion is fundamentally rooted in the sacred invocation of God, a cornerstone of their worship and a powerful testament to their divine covenant. In the depths of anguish and torment, the Psalms resound with fervent pleas to the divine, offering poignant expressions of faith. Divine intervention, a powerful force grants emancipation, His consistent backing instilled a resolute faith, a conviction in His enduring presence.

From a theological perspective, calling upon God transcends mere ceremonial observance; it constitutes a deeply felt testament to faith, a humble reliance on the divine power. This act implicitly recognizes God's ultimate authority and the supplicant's absolute dependence on His boundless mercy and timely intervention. Humility and faith are the bedrock of invocation, a sacred act frequently interwoven with supplication and reverence.

"At that time people began to call upon the name of the Lord."[2] *(Then, people invoked the Lord).*

"Call upon Me in the day of trouble; I will deliver you, and you will honor me."[3] *(Call me in your hour of need; I will save you, and you will praise me).*

God's boundless compassion is most vividly manifested in the passionate reverence we offer. Resolute Faith, piety and an intimate connection with sacred scriptures illuminate the truest path to experiencing divine grace. Ultimately, it is through heartfelt worship that we find ourselves

---

2. Genesis 4:26
3. Psalm 50:15

most closely enveloped in the Almighty's loving presence:

"But from there you will seek the Lord your God and you will find Him, if you search after Him with all your heart and with all your soul."[4] *(Resolute faith in God ignites a radiant revelation of His majesty. A wholehearted, soul-deep yearning ensures a transcendent communion with God Almighty).*

"You will seek me and find me when you seek me with all your heart." (29:13[5] *(Seek me wholeheartedly, and you will find me).*

"Draw near to God, and He will draw near to you."[6] *(Seek God intimacy, and a closeness will reciprocate. Cultivate this sacred connection).*

"God inhabits the praises of His people."[7] *(Psalm 22:3) (The adoration of the faithful is the dwelling place of God).*

God communion, as we have observed, hinges upon a humble and gentle heart Cultivate this attitude; a spirit of receptive heart open heart,

---

4.   Deuteronomy 4:29
5.   Jeremiah 29:13
6.   James 4:8
7.   Psalm 22:3

allowing the Him to permeate your being. Understand the weight of your prayers; Show piety, a passionate tribute born of faith and await the divine blessing that will surely follow. Seek tranquility in a peaceful respite; a refuge of stillness awaits. Foster a centered, reverent spirit, maintain this commitment: invite the God of Most High, welcoming the glory of the Almighty. Contemplate the breathtaking grandeur of the Almighty, enveloped in a luminous, holy aura. Let its radiant energy permeate your very being, filling you with celestial brilliance. Regular recitation of the sacred verse will ignite a brilliant inner light, triggering a quantum leap in your soul. This process transfigures your soul, weaving it into the very essence of the divine.

Commence these sacred prayers by inviting the God Almighty, thankful for His boundless grace. This transcends mere entreaty; it's a consecrated bond, a powerful bulwark against the malignant influence of ancestral or contemporary evil. This powerful incantation forcefully dispels the insidious forces of negativity, clearing the path toward spiritual and emotional renewal. Seeking divine intervention to illuminate the deepest ambitions ensures their potent realization, transforming this sacred pact into an inviolable fortress safeguarding very being. Escape the cacophony of daily life and find sanctuary in a serene haven. Total submersion is crucial; this profound retreat necessitates undivided attention to unlock its transformative potential. Find the sanctuary, fostering inner peace through mindful respiration, connecting with the God. Continue this practice until tranquility washes over you.

"I invoke the Divine Light of the Most High, Expanding Fire Breath of God!" (God's light protects me, Christ's kingdom brings peace, God's might sustain me).

"I Pray Fully to God Almighty, The Ruler of Heaven Who Possesses the Golden Light. My soul yearns for Your closeness. I crave communion with You, worshiping, adoring, and cherishing You with all my heart. Grant my fervent prayer Lord. (To the Almighty, sovereign of the universe, bathed in radiant glory, I offer my heartfelt supplication. My spirit thirsts for your presence, longing for sacred union. I prostrate myself before you, revering your majesty, adoring your boundless grace, and embracing you with devotion. Hear my earnest prayer, O Lord).

Masterful Implementation- Successful Execution:

sacred songs, a gift from God, possess a timeless power that deeply touches the human soul. Explore their transformatory capacity to reshape your life and understand their enduring legacy — an impact that transcends comprehension. Choose the invocations that most resonate with your spirit; let your inspiration guide you to the most emotionally and spiritually powerful selections. Integrate multifaceted therapeutic exercises into each practice session, comprehensively addressing diverse challenges. This holistic approach triggers restoration and healing within each prayerful session. Reciting the divine hymns prayer cultivates a deeper connection with God, we unleash powerful forces that fundamentally reshape our reality. Through dedicated devotion, inherited flaws and insidious spiritual afflictions are purged. This process effects a metamorphosis transmuting these impediments through spiritual regeneration into divine grace; a powerful renewal of the spirit. Even during the moments of serenity, these sacred verses instill vigor and uplift the soul, bestowing enduring fortitude and spirit.

Providing security, they form an invincible barrier, a bastion of steadfast defense, safeguarding you and your cherished family.

Sacred hymns, luminous and blessed, resonated with ethereal power. They resonate with a deeply sacred essence, possessing cosmic authority, its influence pervades all existence, their ethereal harmonies whisper the mysteries of bygone eras, possessing the transformatory capacity to ignite enduring evolution. These powerful verses provide sanctuaries of grace, fostering the unfolding of complete spiritual enlightenment. A yearning thirst for God, a consuming desire for the sublime, Demands complete focus. Pour your resolute commitment into this longing, merging your consciousness with its dazzling power. Envision its celestial luminescence, a radiant, god's splendor guiding your path. A luminous celestial guide illuminates your predestined journey.

Forgiveness

The limitless compassion of self-forgiveness and the pardon of others surpasses all prayers. This selfless humility instantly draws celestial grace, initiating an inner metamorphosis. It purifies your essence—body, mind, and spirit— unleashing a radiant wave of optimism that ripples outward, impacting the world from personal world to the global stage. This powerful, divine force significantly enhances the likelihood of manifesting your most cherished aspirations.

Forgiveness, as depicted in sacred texts, is a profoundly restorative power, a boundless and life-altering gift. We routinely minimize the gravity of forgiveness, allowing the insidious poison of resentment to stealthily undermine our happiness. Unresolved anger, though outwardly calm, casts a malignant shadow over existence. The deep wounds inflicted by betrayal and malice, particularly those ignited by intense fury and a thirst for vengeance, stubbornly resist the gentle healing of pardon. Forgiveness feels not merely unwarranted, but a violation, a desecration of the self. Untreated emotional injuries can consume a life, an unbearable weight until true liberation is found. Painful recollections, persistent as barbed hooks, relentlessly lacerate the spirit, resurrecting past agony with unrelenting savagery. While some might proclaim reconciliation, the scars remain, a stark testament to suffering endured; a constant, visceral ache dwelling in the heart's depths.

An imbalance skews our memory of misdeeds: we vividly remember others' offenses, yet our own failings against them often fade, obscured by self-forgiveness or simply swallowed by the passage of time. This prejudiced recollection is greatly unsettling. Spiritual paths universally emphasize self-examination as the cornerstone of reconciliation; a genuine confession of our culpability—a heartfelt acceptance of our flaws— must precede any plea for restorative justice. A practice entails painstakingly cataloging our own transgressions against others, then juxtaposing this inventory with a record of their wrongs against us. The resulting disparity will be strikingly revealing.

A sobering self-assessment often reveals a painful truth: our inflicted injuries vastly eclipse those we've sustained. This disparity necessitates a rigorous examination of our conduct and its devastating consequences for others. We meticulously tend to our own hurts, conveniently overlooking the grievous offenses we've perpetrated. Yet, the courageous act of pardon represents a conscious allegiance to a superior ethical code, offering immeasurable rewards. Choosing this path unveils a sacred grace, a transformative journey toward spiritual wholeness—God's benediction.

Sacred texts illuminate the boundless spiritual rewards of pardon. Shedding the suffocating shackles of bitterness and wrath unveils a tranquil inner sanctuary. This act of relinquishment frees us from the agonizing burden of past hurts, fostering a serene and enduring tranquility within our souls. The Scripture illuminate the significance of extending forgiveness—both to ourselves and to others—revealing the bountiful grace the Almighty bestows upon those who embrace this transcendent virtue:

"Blessed is the one whose transgressions are forgiven, whose sins are covered." [8] *(Blessed is the*

8. Psalm 32:1

soul whose faults are forgiven, whose sins are veiled in mercy).

"Judge not, and you will not be judged; condemn not, and you will not be condemned; forgive, and you will be forgiven..."[9] *(Don't judge; you won't be judged; don't condemn; you won't be condemned; Pardon, and be pardoned- Forbear judgment, and find mercy).*

Consistent immersion in these sacred texts fosters a deep spiritual connection, nurturing exceptional personal growth and significantly accelerating the realization of ambitious goals. This powerful practice unlocks your innate potential for life-altering progress:

"I am in the Divine Love and Mercy, I am in the Divine Christ Light and Healing, Forgiveness Everywhere!" *(Christ's infinite compassion is my refuge, offering total redemption and pardon).*

"I abide in God's Grace and Blessing, I abide in God's Unity and Harmony, Forgiveness Everywhere!" *(God's grace and faith bring peace; trust anchors my soul in divine harmony and boundless pardon).*

---

9. Luke 6:37

Predestiny: God's Eternal Design

Unveiling our preordained life's work, our ultimate raison d'être, constitutes a formidable spiritual quest. The solution resides exclusively within God, for this knowledge transcends human intellect, a sacred secret held solely by the Almighty. As previously mentioned, certain individuals, inheriting a legacy of grace from their forefathers, are gifted with an innate grasp of their predetermined trajectory, a divinely ordained mission effortlessly unveiled.

In awe of the Holy Trinity, a unified yet distinct Spirit and Person, let us commence our time with fervent devotion, humbly submitting our petitions. Humanity's vision regarding professional paths is tragically limited. Despite parents' painstaking efforts to sculpt their children's destinies, their meticulously crafted blueprints for triumph often yield unforeseen results. The anticipated alignment of aspiration and achievement remains frustratingly, consistently elusive.

Unexpected detours frequently disrupt the meticulously planned trajectories of individual and familial ambitions. The achievement of initial goals offers no guarantee of enduring success; sustaining achievements proves a precarious undertaking. Regardless of academic credentials, the path to mastery is often paved with iterative trials, numerous failures, and hard-won lessons. The unpredictable ebb and flow of existence highlights the crucial importance of cultivating a spirit of humble supplication and boundless empathy, seeking solace and strength in a higher power.

Let us fervently implore divine guidance to light our way toward a life of meaning. Humanity, propelled by an insatiable thirst for more, cherishes a myriad of ambitions. It is the very essence of our being to earnestly seek the gratification of these longings, even while recognizing the inherent uncertainty of realizing our cherished aspirations. The inherent worth of supplication transcends the assurance of a favorable outcome. Embrace the act with unwavering faith, pouring out your soul's deepest desires; anticipate a divine response. However, those forbidden desires, those violations of the established cosmic balance, will inevitably culminate in your predetermined path, molded by the relentless march of time, draws ever closer. Rather than blindly navigating a labyrinth of missteps, fervently implore the Divine for illumination, seeking the revelation of your innate, God-given purpose. The widespread belief that financial success — a lucrative career, perhaps — equates to fulfilling God's ultimate design is a misunderstanding. Ultimately, the revelation of God's intended path unfolds according to its own unyielding, preordained schedule.

Sacred texts declare a divine authorship of individual life paths. The immutable core of each person — a bedrock of unique identity — underpins our collective human experience. Against overwhelming power, defiance proves not merely futile, but catastrophically self-defeating; opposition disintegrates before its unstoppable force:

"Whatever exists has already been named, and what humanity is has been known; no one can contend with someone who is stronger." [10] (Entrust your aspirations to God's steadfast providence, and He will transform your most fervent desires into enduring achievements).

---

10. Ecclesiastes 6:10

"Commit to the Lord whatever you do, and he will establish your plans."[1] *(Commit all your pursuits to God's unwavering care, and He will strengthen your deepest ambitions into unshakeable realities).*

"In him we were also chosen, having been predestined according to the plan of him who works out everything in conformity with the purpose of his will."[2] *(Through him, our destiny was sealed, divinely ordained within the grand design of the One who masterfully orchestrates all things according to the unwavering dictates of His sovereign will).*

Fortune's favors fall unevenly upon humanity. For some, their life's trajectory is clear from the outset; others drift through existence, tragically misusing precious years—even a whole lifespan— in a relentless quest for genuine meaning, yearning for the destiny ordained by a higher power. A spiritual disconnect arises from the relentless pursuit of transient pleasures, a disregard for our core moral obligations and the erosion of heartfelt thankfulness and faith in the Divine.

---

1. Proverbs 16:3
2. Ephesians 1:11

Humanity often disregards the sacred origins of its blessings, remaining tragically unaware of the celestial source from which all bounty flows. Prioritizing fleeting gratifications over one's authentic calling ultimately leads to a desolate and impoverished existence. Time, a relentless thief, pilfers our most valuable years. A grand design, divinely ordained, remains tragically incomplete, leaving an ache of unrealized ambition—a colossal, irretrievable loss. The journey to self-discovery is rarely a straightforward voyage; for countless individuals, it's a turbulent odyssey, a bewildering quest to navigate the treacherous currents of uncertainty and unearth their authentic purpose.

Liberation arrives through heavenly grace. Sacred chants, potent and resonant, will obliterate the malevolent forces that bind you. The deep-seated agony of a lifetime, the crushing weight of past actions, will be completely eradicated. This powerful invocation shatters the wicked chains of suffering, freeing your soul from the insidious spells that hold it captive and a benevolent power shields you from all evil, an unwavering guardian against darkness. Hidden in the core of every being lie a personal blueprint, a destiny's map overflowing with unrealized capabilities, aching for its radiant revelation. A celestial imperative whispers within, compelling the actualization of your unique calling, a magnificent purpose poised to blossom within your ordained domain. Embrace this immutable truth, and unshackle yourself from the soul-crushing burden of hopelessness.

The time has arrived to actively challenge and eradicate the insidious forces hindering your progress, seizing back what has been wrongfully taken. Harness the potent energy of divine grace; otherwise, these inherited, cyclical patterns, deeply embedded within your ancestral lineage, will fester and corrupt your physical, emotional, and spiritual core. This pervasive negativity, if left unchecked, will poison every facet of your existence, perpetuating a cycle of despair. Embrace your sacred destiny, for inaction condemns you to a life of unfulfilled potential and emptiness. Chanting these holy verses unlocks your preordained path, a divinely ordained destiny. Each day, let this sacred invocation resonate within you, fostering an intimate communion with the transcendent. This unwavering devotion will engender extraordinary spiritual evolution, dramatically hastening the realization of your deepest aspirations.

"I abide in God's Master, I abide in God's Inheritance, I abide in God's King's Road of Promise!" (A magnificent future, divinely guided, awaits. My life, blessed and purposeful, unfolds according to God's plan).

"I abide in God's Guidance and Ordinance, I abide in God's formation and predestination!" (Destiny's design, ingrained in my soul, filled my actions with significance, making my life purposeful. I am an integral part of its grand narrative.).

"I abide in God's Way, I abide in God's Truth, I abide in God's Life, Predestined Path and Perfection!" (Guided by faith, I seek enlightenment. My dedicated path, rooted in truth, assures my ultimate triumph. This divine connection pervades my soul.).

"I dwell in God's Wisdom, I dwell in God's Guidance, I dwell in God's Journey of Predestination!" (Dwelling in God's wisdom, I'm guided by a God's plan, my faith fueling each sacred step on my appointed path.).

Abundant Blessings

Inner purity, a soul free from transgression, forms the bedrock of a righteous existence. For most, the path to divine favor hinges on an unspoken agreement: Purifying the soul initiates a outpouring of God's grace, impacting all facets of existence. Therefore, the wisest course is fervent thanksgiving, a ceaseless recognition of the Creator's infinite generosity, the wellspring of all we possess. The eminent theologian, Augustine asserts:

"Blessed are the pure in heart, for they shall see God. Let us make every effort to purify our hearts, exert ourselves to stay alert, and as far as in us lies gain this grace by constant prayer.[3] *(Divine revelation comes only to the devout. Let us pursue spiritual purity, fostering a connection with God through constant prayer).* Similarly, the Scripture attests it's the magnitude of its truth:

"...Blessed are the meek, for they will inherit the earth. Blessed are those who hunger and thirst for righteousness, for they will be filled. Blessed

---

3. Augustine, Sermon 277, p.15-16

*are the merciful, for they will be shown mercy.
Blessed are the pure in heart, for they will see
God. Blessed are the peacemakers, for they will
be called children of God, Blessed are those who
are persecuted because of righteousness, for theirs
is the kingdom of heaven...."*[4] *(The humble inherit
the earth, their gentle strength transforming the world.
Justice-seekers find deep fulfillment. Compassionate
hearts bask in boundless kindness. The pure see divine
glory, forever changing their perspective. Peacemakers,
God's beloved, receive heavenly grace. Those enduring
unjust persecution for righteousness achieve eternal
triumph).*

*"But blessed is the one who trusts in the Lord,
whose confidence (faith) is in him."*[5] *(Fortunate
is the soul that relies upon the Almighty, whose
unshakable faith is anchored in Him).*

*"...but those who hope in the Lord will renew
their strength. They will soar on wings like eagles;
they will run and not grow weary; they will walk
and not be faint."*[6] *(Trusting God renews vitality.*

---

4. Matthew 5:2-10
5. Jeremiah 17:7)
6. Isaiah 40:31

Like eagles, they soar, tireless and indomitable, their strength boundless.).

"Every good gift and every perfect gift is from Above!"[7] *(God's abundant blessings enrich every aspect of life, as scripture confirms. All good gifts come from above).*

"The blessing of the Lord brings wealth, without painful toil for it.!"[8] *(God's grace brings effortless abundance; trust in His limitless provision to meet all your needs).*

"God will supply every need of yours...."[9] *(Divine providence will abundantly fulfill all your needs).*

Regular engagement with these following divine hymns prayer cultivates spiritual intimacy, fostering remarkable self-improvement and dramatically hastening the attainment of challenging aspirations. This powerful practice unleashes your inherent capacity for breathtaking, life-enhancing advancement.

"I abide in God's blessings I abide in God's Purity & righteousness, I am a blessed child of God,

---

7. James 1:17
8. Proverbs 8:29
9. Philippians 4:19

Divine kingdom of heaven & earth!" *(Divine grace surrounds me; I am pure and virtuous, a beloved child of God, inheriting His boundless kingdom).*

I abide in God's mercy & peacemaker, I abide in God's inheritance of perfect gift!" I trust in the Lord of Promiss, With My Constant prayer! *(God's grace and peace are mine; I claim my God's inheritance with relentless prayer).*

Happiness

The yearning for happiness is inherent, a fundamental human drive, mirroring even the apparent contentment of animals. Yet, achieving genuine happiness proves elusive. Life's complexities—personal struggles and global turmoil—frequently cast a shadow, fostering despair and disorientation. The challenge isn't merely attaining happiness, but sustaining it—a lifelong pursuit that even figures of immense faith often found arduous, sometimes achieving lasting contentment only in their twilight years. Many fail to grasp that happiness is a divine endowment, accessible only through a conscious commitment: a journey of companionship with God.

Socrates believed that the key to happiness was to turn attention away from the body and towards the soul. By gaining rational control over desires and harmonizing the different parts of the soul, individuals could achieve a *"divine-like state of inner tranquility"* that external circumstances could not affect. He believed in a higher, divine power concerned with justice and virtue. He also spoke of being guided by an inner divine voice or sign (daimonion), which he interpreted as a form of prophecy. In essence, Socrates believed that true happiness resided within the individual's soul and was connected to a divine force, accessible through virtue, wisdom, and self-examination, leading to inner peace and a life of flourishing (eudaimonia).[10]

Augustine masterfully portrays the elusive nature of true happiness. He argues that this blessed state transcends the merely physical; it's not a tangible thing perceived by the senses, nor is it a simple intellectual capacity like numerical recall: *"...for the happy life is not visible to the eye, since it is not a physical object. Is it the sort of memory we have for numbers....?*[11] *(Our souls remain eternally unsettled until they find solace and ultimate fulfillment in divine communion).* He simply concludes as: *"Restless is our heart until it comes to rest in you."*[12] *(Our souls yearn, unsettled and adrift, until they find solace and peace in Your embrace).*

Augustine believed that ultimate happiness and fulfillment could only be found in God, who

---

10. Jones, R. E. Socrates Bleak View of the Human Condition. 36: 97-105
11. Augustine, Confessions, Book X, Ch. 11
12. Augustine, Confessions, Book I, Ch. 1

is the source of all goodness and the highest good itself. He argued that our hearts are restless until they rest in God. His conception of happiness is deeply intertwined with scriptural teachings, finding therein its consistent validation:

"Take delight in the Lord, and he will give you the desires of your heart."[13] *(Find your joy in the Lord, and He will abundantly fulfill your heart's deepest longings).*

"The Lord is my strength and my shield; my heart trusts in him, and he helps me. My heart leaps for joy, and with my song I praise him."[14] *(The Lord, my strength and shield, sustains my trusting heart, filling it with joyful praise).*

Through devout utterance of the hallowed prayer, you summon the Almighty's sacred essence, achieving a spiritual communion that showers you with divine grace. Persistent recitation cultivates an increasingly intimate connection with the Godhead, generating a potent force for rapid spiritual growth. The intensity and regularity of your supplications directly correlate

13. Psalm 37:4
14. Psalm 28:7

with the depth of transformative blessings you will receive, shaping your life through God's merciful intervention:

"I dwell in God's Perfect Health, I dwell in God's Perfect Wealth, I dwell in God's Perfect Happiness!" (*I dwell in a magnificent realm of unlimited potential, brimming with joy, prosperity, and well-being*).

"I abide in God's Way, I abide in God's Truth, I abide in God's Life, Perfection Manifestation of Divine Spirit!" (*God's radiance unveils creation's glory. I tread the holy way, living truthfully, steadfast in this life-altering pilgrimage, embracing a new life*).

"I reside in God's Love and Harmony, I reside in God's peace and unity, Blessed Being of the Divine Essence!" (*God's peace unlocks inner peace and spiritual healing. My journey starts in sacred unity, fostering deep connections. O magnificent source of all being*).

"I reside in God's Life and Joy; I reside in God's Manifestation!" (*I reside within the heavenly bliss of existence, I embody the radiant expression of the Holy Spirit*).

Love: Divine Decree

Unconditional love—the commandment to cherish one another—surpasses all other cures. It transcends mere retribution, instead embodying a boundless, merciful grace. This God's elixir nurtures, mends, and rejuvenates every facet of existence. It miraculously revitalizes, bestowing enduring youth and radiant beauty, transforming morbid contemplations into vibrant aspirations for life. Through heartfelt affection tempered with self-control, impossibilities yield; the entire essence of one's being is purified and elevated.

A life so deeply interwoven with devotion transcends mere fleeting setbacks; it achieves all within its potential. This understanding reveals love's immense protective power, transmuting hostile intent into blessings. The adversary's malevolence is thus neutralized, their attacks blossoming into the exquisite perfume of roses. Divine benevolence and affection are priceless human assets. Unlock inner potential by reciting the enclosed sacred prayer. Its potent vibrations will amplify this extraordinary gift.

"I resid in God's Love and Sentiment, I resid in God's Compassion, Perfect Demonstration of the God's Love!" (*I dwelled in God's compassion and love, a perfect testament to God's grace*).

"I abide in God's Unity and Harmony, I abide in God's Grace and Mercy, Perfect Demonstration of the Divine benevolence!" (*God's boundless grace envelops me, a refuge of compassion, a testament to His infinite love.*).

Prosperity

The divine essence of prosperity is not found in the pursuit of fleeting pleasures or the accumulation of earthly treasures. Instead, it lies in the cultivation of a prosperous soul—a vessel brimming with gratitude, compassion, and a deep understanding of the divine plan. By aligning our desires with the divine will, we unlock the true source of abundance. This sacred union transforms our lives, empowering us to manifest our deepest aspirations and fulfill our divine purpose. Through the power of prayer and the recitation of the divine hymns prayer, we invite the God of Most High to orchestrate our intentions and guide our actions. This sacred alliance becomes our fortress, protecting us from the insidious grip of negative influences and ancestral curses. With unshakable faith and diligent preparation, we can attract the divine essence of prosperity, manifesting it in our lives and creating a future of limitless abundance.

Ancient philosophies frequently portray affluence and opulence as treacherous pathways leading to moral corruption. Wealth is not inherently evil; indeed, financial prosperity, when guided by prudence, is a powerful force for good. Scripture abounds with numerous illustrative instances. We acutely understand the hardships of a life devoid of resources. However, the misery often attributed to riches stems not from the possession of money itself, but from its misuse – from the corrosive influence of avarice, selfishness, and destructive ambitions. Such actions inevitably deplete one's abundance and removal of God's blessings, both material and spiritual. Even as the various religious and ethical traditions, particularly within the Abrahamic faiths warn, disregard for God's law ultimately leads to injures oneself: ***"One who ignores the Divine Law brings about his own destruction."***[15] The law of cause and effect dictates that rejecting wealth invites its rejection in return. Consequently, attracting abundant prosperity becomes elusive, or if achieved, proves fleeting. An obstacle for the financially challenged lies in their disconnection from a mindset of abundance. Many, particularly within specific professions and among religious zealots, harbor a deeply ingrained belief that

---

15. Anonymous

the love of money is the source of all evil. This disdain for wealth creates a powerful barrier to financial success, effectively obstructing the path to prosperity. Ancient wisdom illuminates this truth: ***"To be prosperous in the outer world, you must be prosperous in the inner world."*** [16] *(External prosperity stems from an unshakeable core of internal wealth).* The perceived dichotomy between the extraordinary and the material realms is illusory; these facets of existence are intrinsically linked, demanding mutual inclusion. A failure to recognize this interdependence inevitably results in a catastrophic breakdown of understanding.

Outdated false dogma associating wealth with wickedness must be discarded; otherwise, financial prosperity will elude you. The undeniable truth is that affluence stems from a deeply ingrained mindset of abundance, while poverty is similarly rooted in a belief of scarcity. If you are attuned to the cosmos, you will intuitively recognize the divine as the ultimate source of your provision. Yield to the boundless, overflowing power of the universe; its miraculous bounty will soon be yours.

---

16. Anonymous

Sacred scripture overflows with passages illuminating the path to abundance. Consider these select verses revealing the God's las of prosperity. These scriptures offer not mere material wealth, but a holistic flourishing – a bountiful life enriched by spiritual blessings and temporal success:

"But You shall remember the Lord your God, for it is He who gives you power to get wealth."[17] *(Acknowledge the Supreme Being, the wellspring of all riches, whose benevolent grace bestows upon you the capacity for boundless prosperity).*

"The blessing of the Lord makes a person rich, and he adds no sorrow with it."[18] *(God's grace brings abundant blessings, free from suffering's cruel hand).*

"Wealth is God's blessing to be enjoyed."[19] *(Prosperity, a divine gift, is meant to be savored and appreciated).*

"Lazy hands make for poverty but diligent hands bring wealth;"[20] *(Prosperity flows from industrious effort; idleness breeds destitution).*

---

17. Deuteronomy 8:18
18. Proverbs 10:22
19. Ecclesiastes 5:18
20. Proverbs 10:4

*"Riches and honor are with me, enduring wealth and righteousnes*s*."*[21] *(Prosperity and acclaim are my constant companions, a legacy of riches and integrity).*

Begin by summoning the divine presence, earnestly beseeching the Source of boundless wealth. Declare your request with faith and heartfelt conviction:

"Golden Light of the Most High, The Light of abundant supply of Divine wealth, It now delivers to me from God Almighty. I now receive the God's Power to draw the eternal abundance and expand my Pre-destined Life. I now follow the heavenly Guidance of the Most High, I petition the perpetual abundance, It is now bestowed upon me by the God Almighty. Let it be manifest now by your Grace!" *(May divine light guide me, granting wisdom and understanding. Heaven's boundless generosity bestows unending wealth and transcendent power, ushering in an era of abundance. God's unwavering hand leads my path, illuminated by His providence. I pray for lasting prosperity, a rich and unending fortune. With gratitude, I accept this heavenly grace. Let your kindness shine brightly).*

---

21. Proverbs 8:18

Embrace tranquility before commencing this God's hymns. Deepening your faith cultivates a bond with the divine, forging a harmonious partnership with the spiritual world. This powerful connection exponentially strengthens the efficacy of your aspirations.

"I now Knock Upon the Door of the Divine Kingdom of Unlimited Prosperity, Let it be Manifest Now!" (*I petition the boundless realm of abundant wealth to open its gates to me. My overflowing prosperity be immediately realized*).

"I reside in God's Unlimited Abundance, I reside in God's Unlimited Resources Manifestation of the Divine Prosperity!" (*Immersed in God's limitless, overflowing mercy, I reside within an inexhaustible, sacred fount of prosperity. Heaven's lavish bounty pours forth endlessly*).

"I abide in God's Pre-destined Abundance, I abide in God's Designed Prosperity, Manifestation of the Divine Fulfillment!" (*I live in a divinely rich land, nurturing its limitless potential. Gratitude breeds abundance, fostering spiritual growth and an awakening*).

Power And Victory

In moments of prosperity and overflowing bounty, Misleading shadows breed doubt, shrouding all in treacherous ambiguity, whispering doubts that could cripple your innate capabilities and derail your predetermined path. Implacable malice, with unwavering determination, relentlessly advances its sinister objective, its grip tightening with inexorable force until its wicked purpose is realized. Ironically, direct confrontation often backfires; attempts to banish these negative influences can inadvertently amplify their power, creating formidable obstacles to success. A self-fulfilling prophecy of failure can easily take root, reinforced by the principle of attraction— negative beliefs draw negative experiences. These destructive patterns, frequently inherited through generations, manifest as recurring, deeply entrenched challenges. To overcome this pervasive negativity, you require a powerful force, a strength surpassing the malevolent powers that relentlessly undermine your life's trajectory.

Only God's intervention can overcome malevolent entities. The supreme, All-Powerful

Being possesses absolute dominion over these evil forces; thus, genuine repentance and spiritual purification are prerequisites to any plea for deliverance. Moved by boundless empathy, the God's responds to heartfelt prayer; passionate plea will eventually shatter the oppressive weight of demonic oppression, freeing you from its evil grip. Having vanquished this spiritual hindrance-a barrier, resolute faith combined with meticulous groundwork for triumph now guides the path, will attract the desired outcome. Conversely, a prayer offered with doubt or hesitation will disrupt the flow of divine energy, potentially self-mastery:

"To be a leader in the outer world, one must be a leader in the inner world."[22] *(Genuine authority emanates not from superficial proclamations, but from an intrinsic core of conviction).*

The Scripture reverberate with a timeless wisdom:

"As a man thinks in his heart, so is he."[23] *(A person's inner landscape mirrors their outward reality. One's internal world shapes their external manifestation).*

---

22. Anonymous
23. Proverbs 23:7

To experience a life overflowing with happiness, cultivate a robust, optimistic perspective—a deep-seated trust in power to mold circumstances. This faith, a God-given conviction, firmly rooted in the subliminal mind provides assurance is the ignition that transforms dreams into lived reality. The Scripture reaffirm this doctrine:

"According to your faith, shall it be done to you."[24] (*Your convictions form the very foundation of your future.*).

Fear and uncertainty, formidable foes, build insurmountable walls around ambition, crippling bold action. These insidious doubts obscure innate genius, threatening to extinguish the true self. Lack of faith, corrodes the spirit, crippling the ability to reach one's full capacity. Dreams take flight only when fueled by unwavering belief and resolute conviction. A celestial grace dispels the soul's hidden terrors, unleashing a potent resurgence of inner strength. Renewed inner strength ignites a metamorphosis, a breathtaking and inspiring odyssey of personal evolution.

---

24. Matthew 9:29

God's grace transcends mere riches; it bestows upon us the sagacity to surmount life's trials and the fortitude to conquer our anxieties. An age-old parable speaks of the unparalleled dominion of the dauntless spirit. ***"One who is fearless, he is absolute."***₂₅ *(He who knows no fear reigns supreme).* Courage, therefore, is ultimate power; nothing is insurmountable for the intrepid heart. Cast off the shackles of a life constrained by apprehension. The Scripture resound with this truth:

"Be brave. Be fearless. You are never alone."₂₆ *(Confront your fears with courage; know that you are inherently connected to something larger than yourself. This unwavering conviction will guide your path).*

Dedication to sacred prayer will gradually erode the debilitating grip of fear and uncertainty. The incantations of these divine hymns act as a powerful counterforce, steadily neutralizing the insidious power of malevolent entities that formerly held your spirit in captive. Scripture reveals that God is the wellspring of miracles—not merely external acts of intervention, but inner manifestations born of faith and unwavering

---

25. Anonymous
26. Joshua 1:9

trust. Deep within the soul's radiant core lies the genesis of daily miracles. Reciting these sacred hymns fosters a communion with God, unleashing a cleansing torrent that purges the nesting corruption within. This devotion will strengthen your spiritual bond, exponentially accelerating the realization of your heart's deepest aspirations. Embrace this transformative practice; let it become the very essence of your being:

"I Knock on the Door of the Divine Kingdom, Of Unlimited Divine Essence, Let it be Manifest now, Let ms be Victorious now!" (From the divine source, I implore a clear sign. My soul, yearning for truth, seeks undeniable proof of your power. Grant me, now, a decisive victory).

"I resid in God's Unlimited Being, I resid in God's Unlimited Potential, Manifest Perfection of Divine Essence!" I dwell at the heart of the divine, inherently one with the infinite Godhead. My existence is boundless potential, a wellspring of endless growth and creation, mirroring God's radiant glory.

"I am in the Divine Splendor, I am in the Divine Wonder, Perfect Expression of Divine Miracles!" (I live in God's radiant glory, fostering a deep connection

and showing the path. This divine bond inspires reverence. I am a perfect reflection of God's sublime creation).

"I abide in God's Destined Path, I abide in God's Destined Action, I abide in God's Destined Manifestation." *(Destiny's immutable design perfectly shapes my life. This unshakeable faith directs my every step, confidently embracing my predestined journey. My future is sealed).*

Life's obstacles are poised for swift and complete annihilation; heartfelt yearnings will soon materialize. A connection with the Supreme Being elicits immediate, breathtaking results. Cultivate a vigilant, receptive spirit, embracing the benevolent currents of existence. **"In order to enter into the Divine Kingdom of abundance, you must keep the child at heart."**[27] *(The path to a realm of overflowing prosperity demands the preservation of childlike wonder and enduring faith).*

Cultivate a heart brimming with happiness and eager expectation, greeting every instant with a deep-seated conviction that it harbors untold grace.

---

27. Mark 10:15

Charisma

Ignite the divine fire residing within your soul and accept God's boundless grace. Seize this divinely bestowed chance, a gift from the heavens, allows you to align your loftiest ambitions with the power of the God's Hymns prayer. By engaging in this practice—a sacred union of your spirit with the divine source—you exponentially increase the manifestation of your heart's deepest longings. This powerful invocation will form a stronger connection with the Almighty, leading to a life-altering metamorphosis:

"I abide in God's Alpha and Omega, I abide in God's Omnipotence!" I abide in God's Light of Supremacy!" (*I dwell within the boundless, primordial source and ultimate end, the omnipotent and sovereign power. I am bathed in the radiant, transcendent glory of supreme authority.*).

"I abide in God's Power and Action, I abide in God's Charisma and Magnetism!" Demonstration of Divine Chosen One!" (*I embody divine power and dynamic force. I radiate heavenly charisma and irresistible allure. My existence is a testament to divine selection and purpose*).

"I abide in God's Magnet and Attraction, I abide in God's Charisma and Fascination, Demonstration of the Divine Power and Success!" (My presence exudes an irresistible enchantment, a cosmic pull that captivates. I apply God's power, my deeds echoing with majestic accomplishment and undeniable success).

I reside in God's Essence, I reside in God's Radiance, I reside in God's Magnificence!" (I dwell within the sacred core, I bathe in the celestial glory, I am encompassed by transcendent splendor.).

By cultivating a deep communion with God, amplify the resonant force of heaven's hymns. Find your center before voicing these holy words; achieve a tranquil stillness through measured, conscious breathing, thereby soothing the turbulence of mind and spirit, and embracing peace. Then, a radiant, empathetic energy will infuse you, transforming your being—body, mind, and soul. This will unveil a higher understanding, guiding your journey with illuminating wisdom, inspiring powerful and purposeful action in all that you do. Let this sublime ideal reshape your very essence.

Youth, Beauty, Eternal Life

Humanity's timeless yearning for eternal youth, captivating beauty, and unending life, reflected in our spiritual aspirations reveals a remarkable inner strength: the power to cultivate an enduring image of timeless elegance and irresistible charm. Through God's infinite compassion, resolute faith in Christ grants life's transformation, alters destinies with redemption. The grip of mortality loosens; this unshakeable conviction, a sacred endowment, resides deep within our souls, conquers death itself.

God's providence is lavishly depicted as the source of all bounty in the scriptures; within the Almighty's benevolent embrace, every aspect of human life—the body, mind and the soul—finds its ultimate purpose and ultimate meaning. Only God's intervention can bestow the extraordinary blessings of reversing the aging process- restored vitality, beauty, and extended life.

These are wonders surpassing human comprehension, manifestations of God's infinite majesty and compassion. Sacred writings deeply intertwine artistic mastery with the divine, depicting the Creator as the ultimate source of existence and breathtaking beauty. A deep, abiding relationship with God is the source of vibrant health, enduring appeal, and exceptional lifespan; these are gifts granted to those who earnestly reflect God's magnificence in their being:

"God gives power to the faint and increases strength for those who have none.... Those who trust in the Lord will find new strength, symbolized by soaring like eagles, running without weariness, and walking without fainting."[28] (*God's* grace fortifies the faithful, granting them indomitable spirit and courage. They soar, *above adversity, eagle-like, their spirit unconquerable*).

"I can do all this through Him who gives me strength"[29] (*His grace enables me to accomplish all things*).

"My flesh shall be fresher than a child's: I shall return to the days of my youth."[30] (*I will revert to the exuberance of my youth exceedingly even the purest bud of infancy*).

---

28. Isaiah 40: 29; 31
29. Philippians 4:13
30. Job 33:25

"He fills my life with good things. My youth is renewed like the eagle's![31] *(He revitalizes my life, renewing me like an eagle).*

True beauty, as holy scriptures illuminate, emanates from a soul deeply cultivated, a spiritual awakening, and an intimate communion with the transcendent. From God's viewpoint, true beauty isn't an ephemeral beauty; rather, it embodies the unchanging elegance of an ancient olive tree, a powerful emblem of perseverance, fortitude, and persistent abundance. Consequently, the divine comprehension of beauty's intrinsic essence constitutes God's ultimate vision of true loveliness.

"His shoots shall spread, and his beauty shall be like the olive tree..."[32] *(Like an olive tree, his branches will flourish, his splendor unmatched, enduring and magnificent).*

"...My Spirit will not contend with humans forever, for they are mortal; their days will be a hundred and twenty years."[33] *(My ethereal essence will not forever wrestle with their ephemeral lives; therefore, humanity's fleeting existence* Limited to

---

31. Psalm 103:5
32. Hosea 14:6
33. Genesis 6:3

a meager 120 years, a fleeting blink in the grand sweep of time.

While the prevailing scholarly interpretation identifies the biblical 120 years as a divine reprieve granted to the wicked generation preceding Noah's flood—a period not explicitly signifying a universal lifespan limit—alternative perspectives posit that this figure represents a potential, eventual average human lifespan. Though uncommon, divine providence in sacred texts reveals instances of exceptional lifespan extension, miraculously restoring life to the deceased—a preternatural power wielded long before the concept of mortality's finality was fully understood:

"...I have heard your prayer; I have seen your tears. Behold, I will add fifteen years to your life."[34] *(Your prayer has reached me, your anguish witnessed. Fifteen years shall be granted unto you, an extension of your earthly sojourn).*

"Then He said to me, 'Prophesy to these bones and say to them, 'Dry bones, hear the word of the LORD! This is what the Sovereign LORD says to these bones: I will make breath enter you, and

---

34. Isaiah 38:5

you will come to life. I will attach tendons to you
and make flesh come upon you and cover you with
skin; I will put breath in you, and you will come
to life. Then you will know that I am the LORD.'
So I prophesied as I was prophesying, there was
a noise, a rattling sound, and the bones came
together, bone to bone. I looked, and tendons and
flesh appeared on them and skin covered them,
but there was no breath in them. Then He said
to me, 'Prophesy to the breath; prophesy, son of
man, and say to it, this is what the Sovereign
LORDS says: Come, breath, from the four winds
and breathe into these slain, that they may live.'
So I prophesied as he commanded me, and breath
entered them; they came to life and stood up on
*their feet-a vast army."*₃₅ *(God commanded me to*
prophesy to dry bones, promising to fill them with
breath, flesh, and life, proving His power. My prophecy
caused the bones to reassemble, but remained lifeless
until, at God's command, I summoned the breath of
life. Instantly, a mighty army arose).

Unleash your inner potential for profound
spiritual advancement through the transformative
power of this sacred prayer.

---

35. Ezekiel 37: 1-14

"I abide in God's eternal beauty, I abide in ageless grace of God's eternal youth. I live eternally in God, immortal manifestation of God's very being!" (Residing in God's timeless splendor, I am an immortal reflection of the divine, eternally youthful and ever-present.).

"I reside in God's Love and Harmony, I reside in God's Regeneration and Rejuvenation!" (God's boundless love transforms me, renewing my very essence. May divine glory shine through me, blessing all I encounter.).

Light: A Source of Rejuvenation

Within our sensory perceptions resides a divine essence, a radiant connection to the source of all creation. Yet, the insidious darkness of negative emotions threatens to extinguish this inner light. As this sacred fire dims beneath the weight of despair and darkness, the potential for physical suffering intensifies. Our paramount challenge, then, is to transmute these potent forces of destruction. By cultivating a connection with God, we can transmute negativity into vibrant well-being, reaping immeasurable rewards for both body and soul.

Sacred texts frequently employ the radiant metaphor of light to represent God's benevolent guidance and the enduring flame of hope. The verses that follow brilliantly illuminate the power of this divine radiance. They offer a message of confidence, assuring us that God's omnipresent truth will ultimately triumph over all darknesses. This powerful divine force transcends the oppressive grip of darkness, serving as a model for God's devoted followers to emulate. These believers are called to radiate God's inherent goodness and boundless love, becoming luminous examples that beckon others towards the divine. The scriptures unveil the solace and unwavering protection afforded by God's sheltering presence. They establish the Bible as an indispensable compass, guiding our steps along life's intricate path. Finally, the sacred writings envision a glorious future where God's resplendent glory shall serve as the ultimate, unyielding source of illumination and enlightenment:

"The light shines in the darkness, and the darkness has not overcome it."[36] *(Luminosity pierces the darkness, darkness's grip has failed to extinguish its radiant divine flame).*

"You are the light of the world…Let your light shine before others, so that they may see your good works…."[37] *(Your genius lights the way. Share your gifts, inspiring a better tomorrow for everyone. Let your greatness shine, motivating others to build a lasting legacy).*

"The Lord is my light and my salvation…."[38] *(God is my guiding radiance and my ultimate deliverance)*

36. John 1:5
37. Matthew 5:14-16
38. Psalm 27:1

"You word is a lamp to my feet and a light to my path."[39] *(Your guidance is my guiding light, showing the path ahead).*

"You, Lord, keep my lamp burning; my God turns my darkness into light."[40] *(Eternal God, you nourish my spirit, turning life's darkness into light).*

"While I am in the world, I am the light of the world."[41] *(My earthly sojourn is a radiant beacon, casting light upon all existence).*

"Then God said, 'Let there be light'; and there was light."[42] *(Subsequently, the Almighty decreed illumination, and instantly, a radiant brilliance emerged).*

Divine Light, a heavenly gift, it bolsters resilience and instills a sense of peace, piercing the shadows of our deepest despair. Its powerful, life-altering force washes away the impurities, leaving spirits and bodies cleansed and renewed, thus banishing anguish and agony. Within this radiant, divine luminescence, we discover the

---

39. Psalm 119:105
40. Roman 12:2
41. John 9:5
42. John 11:25

resilience to conquer adversity and embrace renewed vigor and meaning. Prayer's power knows no limits, especially when spoken with unshakeable conviction and heartfelt piety, the words carry weight. Invoking the Divine opens us to immeasurable blessings. Each supplication wraps us in a haven of solace, shielding us from life's tumultuous storms and guiding us toward a future brimming with hope and limitless potential.

While science validates the constant, low-level nuclear processes within us, these atomic interactions are insignificant compared to an effect of devout prayer. This sacred act, a gift from the divine, acts as a powerful accelerant, igniting a transfiguring energy that saturates our being—physical, mental, and spiritual—resulting in a transcendent state of blissful oneness. This sublime experience surpasses the limitations of mortality, offering a glimpse into a realm unbound by earthly constraints. The renowned fifteenth-century Swiss physician and theologian, Paracelsus, proclaimed: healing emanates from God, luminous energy. This celestial effulgence, a gift from the Creator is a wellspring of boundless peace and protection, offering comfort to the afflicted and illuminating the pathway to spiritual rebirth. Its pristine, vigorous power purifies and cleanses, banishing the darkness of disease, anguish, and misery. A beacon of hope, this radiant force lifts the despairing soul to a plane of vibrant well-being and renewed life:

"Everything that lives in light; everything that has an existence radiates light. All things that derive their life from light and this light, in its root are life itself."[43] *(Radiant healing energy, a divine gift, offers peace, strength, and spiritual renewal. Its potent purity cleanses, dispelling suffering and guiding toward vibrant health and hope).*

Accept this fundamental reality: it forms the very core of existence. Indifference yields readily to proactive engagement, empowering you with the resolute will to triumph over any obstacle. Seek the Almighty's benevolent grace; implore His divine intervention to shower you with blessings. This will kindle a fervent resurgence of zeal and fervor revitalizing your entire being.

---

43. Paracelsus, De Natura Rerum, Comp. by John French. Aula Lucis Press, London, UK

"I dwell in God's Essence, I dwell in God's Radiance, I dwell in God's Magnificence, demonstration of God's Miracle!" (I exist within its ethereal glow, committed to this sacred journey. The Almighty's transcendent majesty enfolds me completely, a testament to the awesome power of God's creation).

I abide in the God's Light of the Most High, A Powerful Expression of the Healing!" (Illuminated by God's resplendent grace, my resolute faith stands as a powerful testament to divine renewal).

"I abide in God's Sacred Light, "I abide in God's Eternal Fire, "I abide in the Supreme Light of the Most High A Powerful Expression of Divine Spirit!" (I am God's radiant essence, my faith my very core. This divine connection is my life, a pilgrimage toward the Almighty, a powerful, unfolding expression of creator).

Healing

Violet, in the celestial sphere, holds ultimate sway—a color embodying God majesty, sovereign power, unparalleled sagacity, and a peaceful stillness. It is the very quintessence of the Christ spirit, filled with powerful restorative forces. Its resonance echoes throughout scripture, notably within the Old Testament, alongside red and blue, forming a sacred triad. Violet embodies life's vibrant force, dynamism, and spiritual power, capable of penetrating the soul, acting as a restorative remedy for ancestral and malevolent influences. This color possesses a remarkable rejuvenating capacity, a resurrection born of the Christ essence, revitalizing souls depleted of spiritual vitality. Harnessing the transformative power of violet, imbued with the Christ essence, allows for the transmutation of mental, physical, and spiritual afflictions into a blissful state of being. Daily recitation of a divine invocation, coupled with communion with the God's Spirit, amplifies this effect, accelerating the manifestation of shift:

"I reside in God's Breath of Healing, I reside in God's Essence of Restoration, I reside in God's Path of Rejuvenation, Ageless, Deathless Manifestation of the Divine Essence!" (God's healing power revitalizes me, a sacred renewal igniting my being. This life-affirming path anchors me in vibrant restoration, bathed in God's light).

Chain of Ancestral Misery

Throughout history, sages have unanimously identified the wellspring of human suffering. The Scripture and philosophical treatises across cultures echo this timeless truth: selfish desires and actions are the fertile ground from which misery sprouts, regardless of whether those seeds were sown by lineage or cultivated anew by individual choices. Universal law, the inexorable principle of cause and effect, dictates that whoever plants the seeds of sorrow will inevitably reap a harvest of pain, either in this lifetime or the next. Indeed, the age-old narrative of human anguish finds its primordial echo in the very dawn of creation myths, such as the Genesis account.

Universal causality dictates that every consequence stems from a precise and foreseeable antecedent. Conversely, each action generates a specific and predictable outcome. This inviolable principle—input invariably yielding output—governs all existence, extending beyond humanity to encompass the cosmos and all its phenomena. Consequently, deeply ingrained beliefs, whether positive or negative, act as potent magnets, attracting similar circumstances and perpetuating a self-fulfilling cycle. This relentless repetition continues until conscious intervention breaks the chain of cause and effect, liberating you from this deterministic loop.

Divine justice reigns supreme, both in the heavens and on Earth. Defying the divine mandates of the Almighty triggers a catastrophic system failure, a cosmic short circuit. The consequences of transgression inevitably catch up with the offender; initial penalties rapidly escalate into an insurmountable burden of karmic debt, potentially leading to irreversible ruin. Even celestial beings, lesser gods and angels, face expulsion and imprisonment for such infractions. Selfishness, coupled with the persistent cultivation of malevolent emotions – hatred, bitterness, dread, rage, envy – is akin to ceaselessly sowing seeds of darkness, consuming the putrid fruit of your own making. Ultimately, you become the embodiment of that very corruption.

Biblical wisdom reveals that hurling condemnation, maledictions, or scathing rebukes upon another is akin to assaulting them with a brutal axe, lacerating them with a poisoned blade, or piercing them with a venom-tipped dart. These malevolent projectiles, once launched, inevitably boomerang with devastating force, inflicting upon the originator a retribution far exceeding the initial cruelty inflicted. Cultivate empathy for your detractors; cherish understanding towards those who challenge you. Let compassion be your guiding principle in navigating conflict, fostering reconciliation, and building bridges across divides.

"…Love your enemies,…" a sacred mandate of immense depth, requires enduring dedication and a steadfast heart, nurtured by constant communion with God. Initially, the uninitiated may react with derision, dismissing the concept as utterly absurd. However, even this skepticism melts away under the potent influence of sacred songs. The resonance of these fervent prayers instantaneously stills the tide of hateful rhetoric, silencing opposition completely.

This transformative, sacred elixir neutralizes all discord and destruction, fostering a blissful state of being and circumstance. Should judgment or condemnation arise, instantly invoke sacred hymns to quell and banish any malevolent influence, preventing the insidious seeding of similar negativity within the soul. Daily, intone this divine blessing to forge an unbreakable bond with the Supreme Spirit, amplifying its potent transformative power for manifestation.

"I abide in God's Forgiveness and Mercy, I abide in God's Purification, Perfect Transformation of Divine Grace!" (God's boundless clemency and pardon are my unwavering refuge. I dwell within the radiant glow of divine cleansing, undergoing a glorious metamorphosis through the grace of the Almighty).

"I reside in God's Essence, I reside in the Alpha and Omega!" (I dwell at the universe's heart, an eternal observer of its evolution. This perspective grants me the very core of existence).

"I abide in God's Resurrection,I abide in God's Rejuvenation, Perfect Expression of Eternal Life!" (My spirit is reborn, a faith journey revealing my immortal core. A sacred transformation illuminates my soul's true essence).

"I abide in God's New Life, I abide in God's Immortality, Perfect Transformation of Divine Essence!" (Resurrected, I walk the holy path, divinely empowered on a journey of faith to ultimate knowledge. Immortality is my eternal haven).

Unresolved negative emotions fester within the deepest being, attracting further negativity—toxic relationships and unfortunate circumstances—unless actively addressed. These inner demons will relentlessly manifest as obstacles in life. To counteract this, invoke the sacred hymns; this prayer acts as a conduit for divine grace, transforming inner turmoil into strength and blessing with positive outcomes. Drawing upon an ancient maxim, Paracelsus asserted that positive thoughts, virtuous speech, and benevolent actions cultivate robust mental, physical, and emotional well-being.[44]

History consistently reveals a profound truth: *"It is a man's kindly acts that are remembered of him in the years after his life."*[45] *(A person's legacy rests not on achievements, but on the enduring resonance of their compassionate deeds).* Therefore, continue planting a seed of peace and harmony; it is the foundation of long-lasting success and fulfillment.

---

44. Paracelsus. De Natura Rerum, Comp. by John French. Aula Lucis Press, London, UK
45. *Ptah-hotep*

Life's inequities, moreover, find a compelling rationale in the immutable hand of destiny:

"As you give, so shall you receive."[46] *(Every act of giving is a reciprocal exchange, an offering to a part of own being reflected outward).*

Every act of giving is a reciprocal exchange, an offering to a part of own being reflected outward. Positive contributions generate a virtuous cycle, amplifying success and joy in your life. Conversely, malevolent actions, fueled by dark intentions, inevitably rebound with intensified negative consequences, inflicting the greatest harm upon the originator. This bromelain principle, the Law of Cause and Effect, typically manifests within a single lifetime; however, its repercussions can sometimes resonate through subsequent generations, impacting descendants.

---

46. Luke 6:38

Destroy Satanic Roots

Is it possible to purge the deep-seated, historical depravity embedded within this malevolent inheritance? Given that, what strategies can effectively curb its unrestrained expansion? Tracing our lineage is a monumental undertaking, comparable to meticulously reassembling a fragmented mosaic. Comprehensive genealogical archives, such as those meticulously maintained within Jewish sacred texts, are exceptionally uncommon. Yet, ignoring the implications of these subliminal, ancestral echoes—these soul-deep memories that inflict suffering and perpetuate a malevolent, ancient curse—is a perilous gamble. Their grip on our lives demands our urgent attention. This infernal residue proves impervious to dissolution, a persistent stain upon the soul, relentlessly evoking the specter of past transgressions. Dante's unyielding principle of divine recompense, a relentless journey toward the Almighty, unfolds allegorically in *Inferno*. There, the soul confronts its inherent wickedness, actively repudiating its transgressions and embracing a path of redemption.[47] This inescapable judgment, a fiat of divine justice, casts a crippling shadow over the sinner's very being. Only by shattering the bonds of law of nature indebtedness—by decisively breaking free from this cycle of eternal suffering—can liberation be achieved.

The immutable Law of Retribution, a decree of God justice, is inescapable, its power often crippling the victim's existence. Liberation lies solely in severing the chains of causal entanglement, thus breaking free from the cycle of unending torment. This powerful elixir of affirmation, readily accessible anytime, anywhere, provides ongoing sustenance for a positive mindset and outlook. The God's hymns prayer penetrates the deepest recesses of malevolent, entrenched forces; yet, certain demonic influences, especially those stemming from ancestral curses, exhibit formidable strength, deeply embedded within the subliminal mind Successful application eradicates lifelong emotional anguish, adversity, and despair – dismantling the pervasive unhappiness caused by cyclical satanic afflictions and inherited burdens that shattering the cage of your suffering.

---

47. *Dante, Malebolge (cantos VIII).*

Persistent, insidious negative thoughts readily infiltrate and colonize the soul, wielding considerable influence over our inner being. To counteract this insidious dominion, we must actively cleanse our minds, bodies, and spirits. Daily recitation of sacred hymns prayers serves as a potent antidote, its cumulative effect amplifying the inherent power of God's grace, progressively purifying our essence.

To reap a bountiful harvest of triumph and achievement, cultivate the fertile soil of your soul with the seeds of God's essence. Nourish these aspirations through fervent prayer and the resonant recitation of sacred hymns, deeply connecting with the transcendent spirit of the Almighty. This communion accelerates the materialization of your heartfelt desires, transforming them into vibrant reality.

Before embarking on prayer, safeguard your spiritual space. Invigorate it with the protective, violet radiance of the Christ's divine essence, a crucial precursor to potent recitation. Neglecting this preparation exposes your positive attributes to malevolent forces, potentially eclipsing your endeavors and rendering them unproductive.

The process, if improperly approached, can attract negativity like iron filings to a magnet, even within a divinely-guided pursuit, leading to entanglement with harmful influences and individuals. Instead, focus your recitations upon God's ordained blueprint – the seed of your intention – to guarantee a bountiful, fruitful outcome. This concentrated approach ensures a far more effective manifestation of your goals.

Liberation from malevolent spiritual influence unlocks rapid ascension to your inherent greatness. Cast off all shackles of self-doubt and limiting beliefs. The path of enlightenment involves unwavering faith in the Supreme Being, invoking the divine power of the Almighty to permeate both your conscious and subliminal minds.

Persistent, troubling issues stem from deep-seated sources: unresolved traumas manifested as recurring nightmares and crippling anxieties, coupled with the toxic impact of certain relationships and inherited family patterns. We must excavate these malevolent roots to achieve lasting resolution. These troubles, deeply rooted in malevolent forces, demand a spiritual communion before invoking the sacred hymns prayer. Deep serenity unlocks a sacred bond with the divine; a potent, ethereal current will then surge through your very essence.

In moments of serenity, before the divine hymns' prayer, summon the violet radiance of Christ's protective power. This sacred invocation, preceding your prayer, will synergistically merge your spirit with the Divine, amplifying the potency of your spiritual manifestations. Embrace this practice consistently:

"I invoke the Christ Light of the Most High Expanding Holy Breath of God!" (Prayer, a sacred fire, purifies, strengthens faith, and ignites compassion. God's grace empowers my soul).

Focus your awareness on the radiant, violet luminescence of Christ's celestial healing power. As you commune with the Almighty, intone these sacred verses, surrendering fully to God's essence. A spiritual rebirth has reshaped life, guiding along a path of unshakable faith and transformation. This sacred pilgrimage, a metamorphosis of the soul, instills inner tranquility and vibrant vitality:

"I abide in God's Resurrection, I abide in God's Rejuvenation, I abide in God's Salvation!"

(Spiritual sanctuary grants freedom and lasting salvation, a revelatory path to ultimate redemption).

"I dwell in God's Law and Order, I dwell in God's Justice and Grace, I now Cut the Chain of Satanic Causation with faith in Christ!" *(Guided by unwavering faith in Christ and a respect for the God's law and order, I resolutely shatter the insidious grip of evil).*

Cease this sequence with solemn gravity, I decree the following unshakeable mandate: By God's providence, let us gratefully accept and utilize this extraordinary gift.

Inner peace, once attained, obviates further recitation. However, deeply rooted consequential burdens, inherited from malevolent ancestors, cling with unrelenting tenacity. enduring devotion, a sacred and personal connection with the ultimate divine, maximizes spiritual efficacy. Therefore, persistent supplication exponentially enhances the celestial power of the sacred chants. Prompt intervention against malevolent forces yields superior outcomes. Addressing nascent threats before their escalation ensures a decisive advantage. Swift action guarantees success, transforming your intervention into a potent force – a golden bough, a conduit of miraculous change. Consistent application of this strategy empowers you, dismantling entrenched, satanic strongholds and leveling the foundations of ancient, oppressive structures. Clarity of mind unlocks serenity and a joyful appreciation for life's richness. With newfound perception, you stand poised at the threshold of limitless potential, ready to embrace a future brimming with exciting possibilities.

Uproot Deadly Growth

Malignant growths, both inherited and personally acquired, inflict trauma, their devastating ripple effects echoing through generations and festering within the afflicted bod; these nesting growths, akin to volatile, suppressed volcanoes are nourished by the toxic residue of harrowing experiences, a ceaseless, agonizing spiral of affliction, expressing itself through debilitating illness. The effects are devastating; a chain reaction of cause and effect where deeply ingrained memories relentlessly poison the system. Sacred texts starkly reveal the agonizing truth of inherited sin: God's righteous judgment, a relentless and unforgiving fury, casts its shadow across countless lineages.

"You shall not bow down to (idols)...I, the Lord your God, am a jealous God, punishing the children for the sin of the parents to the third and fourth generation of those who hate me...;" [48] *(God's wrath, a righteous fire, consumes the sins of ancestors, burning through generations — their children, grandchildren,*

---

48. Exodus 20:5-6

and beyond—a devastating consequence for those who brazenly reject His authority).

"So also I will make you sick...."[49] *(I shall inflict upon you a debilitating affliction).*

A positive outlook fosters robust cellular well-being. Sacred texts urge us to relinquish worry, instead approaching all concerns through prayerful petition and gratitude. Ignoring this vital truth permits the insidious growth of illness, even cancer, to spread unrestrained. Divine hymns prayer possesses a great capacity for renewal, offering a route to wholeness. This divine essence, filled with a grace of the divine unconditional love, enables us to overcome ingrained weakness and cultivate a life richer in purpose and well-being. The Scripture offer compelling evidence supporting this claim:

"...but showing love to a thousand generations of those who love me and keep my commandments"[50] *(My affection, however, extends to countless generations of devoted adherents who cherish and uphold my precepts).*

---

49. Micah 6:13
50. Exodus 20:5-6

"He will not die for his father's sin; he will surely live"[51] *(His father's transgression will not claim his life; his existence is assured).*

"...If you pay attention to his commands and keep all his decrees, I will not bring on you any of the diseases...."[52] *(Strict adherence to God's commands, obedience to every sacred decree, will shield you from the devastating onslaught of disease).*

The luminous compassion of Christ cleanses the spirit, while God's hymns infuse the soul with healing grace, revitalizing its very core. Harmonizing one's being with the divine essence transforms the subliminal mind, cultivating a tranquil awareness. This shift banishes inner shadows, fostering a profound and abiding serenity:

"I abide in God's Blessing and Thanksgiving, I abide in God's Favor and Protection, I abide in God's Youth, and Revitalization! *(I am enveloped in a sea of blessings, a holy shower of mercy. God's protection enfolds me, a radiant shield against life's storms. My spirit undergoes a breathtaking renewal;*

---

51. Ez.18:17b
52. Exodus 15:26

a vibrant, youthful energy surges within, flourishing like a spring bloom).

"I reside in God's Purity, I reside in God's Restoration, I reside in God's Revival!" *(I dwell in sacred peace, my heart pure and devoted to holiness. A spiritual renewal sweeps over me, my faith unwavering. I walk a path of holy restoration, a pilgrimage of rebirth).*

Freedom from Malignant Triad: Fear, Doubt and Jealousy—A Soul Corroding Substance

Fear, suspicion, and the bitter poison of jealousy intertwine in the agonizing waltz of love, a destructive spiral that obscures happiness and breeds inner turmoil. Jealousy, the most formidable enemy of affection, festers in the recesses of the mind, a merciless tyrant that afflicts both individual and beloved. However, this insidious weed can be uprooted through diligent cultivation of spiritual principles. Reciting the divine hymns prayer infuses the subliminal mind with a powerful surge of God's essence, offering solace and spiritual renewal. This enriching process cultivates creative power; inspiring groundbreaking ideas and a life filled with meaningful intention. It ensures a lasting transmutation of the soul, banishing doubt and replacing it with love and harmony.

"I abide in God's Love and Compassion, I abide in God's Mercy and Forgiveness, I abide in God's Grace and blessing (God's infinite mercy sustains

my spiritual path, a boundless flood of forgiveness and love. I am empowered by His grace.).

"I reside in God's Faith with Conviction, I reside in God's Adoration and Admiration, I reside in God's Wisdom and guidance!" *(God's unwavering grace illuminates my life, guiding and inspiring me as a vessel of divine wisdom.).*

The act of relinquishing control over something saps its potency. Similarly, a self-effacing ego, unburdened by narcissistic introspection, inevitably decays from its own inherent weakness. When transcend the sting of an adversary's malevolence, their cruelty becomes impotent. This dynamic, the inherent principle of duality, guarantees its inevitable resolution.

End of Misery

Interpersonal strife and the venomous emotions it breed—loathing, bitterness, and desolation—poison every aspect of life. These corrosive feelings shatter inner peace, erecting formidable barriers to happiness and advancement. A mind uncluttered by negativity allows inherent potential and positive energies to thrive, naturally directing focus toward productive pursuits. Sadly, many unknowingly sow the seeds of their own suffering, carefully cultivating them into agonizing realities. To attain genuine fulfillment, one must consciously replace ingrained, self-limiting beliefs with empowering visions of prosperity and spiritual grace. Breaking free from the shackles of painful past experiences initiates a healing, affecting both the conscious and unconscious realms. The daily invocation of sacred prayers, accompanied by an awareness of the Divine, ignites a transformative journey, culminating in miraculous results.

"I abide in God's Healing I abide in God's Restoration, Perfect Demonstration of Divine

Grace! And Mercy" (*A spiritual journey has reborn me, revealing God's boundless love and compassion*).

"I abide in God's Remedy I abide in God's Purification, Perfect Demonstration of Divine Totality" (*Divine power cleanses and transforms me, resurrecting my spirit within sacred renewal*).

"I reside in God's Love and Harmony, Expression of God's Law of Grace and Mercy!" (*Radiant love envelops me, fostering inner peace and transforming my life. God's boundless compassion and forgiveness illuminate my way*).

"I abide in God's Protection, I abide in God's Custody, I abide in God's Guardianship!" (*God's unwavering grace shelters me; His mercy, an impenetrable fortress against all harm*).

Cited

(PREFACE)
Ancient Doctrine-Unanimous
Genesis 11:6

(PART I)
Plotinus
Isaiah 40:21-22; 28
1Corinthians 15:40-58 1 Corinthians 15:40-58
Manly P. Hall, (re-print-2007) Saint-Germain.
    Kessinger Publishing
Manly P. Hall, (re-print-2007) Saint-Germain.
    Kessinger Publishing
Manly P. Hall. (1963) The most holy
    trinosophia of the Comte de St. Germain,
    The philosophical research society, inc.
William Doyle. (1989) The Oxford History of
    the French Revolution, Oxford Univ. Press.
Alison M. Roberts (2019) Hathor's Alchemy:
    The ancient Egyptian Roots of the Hermetic
    art. Northgate Publishers

(PART II)
Augustine, From discourse on the Psalms,
    Psalm 37, 13-14, pp.391-392
Albert Einstein: the quote
Ancient wisdom: Anonymous
Betegh, Gabor, Pythagoreans, Orphism and
    Greek Religion, in Huffman 2014a,.149-157

Colossiens 1:15-17

Deutéronome 28:11

Deutéronome 31:6

Ecclésiastes 3:7

Ephésiens 3:16

Ephesians 3:20

Ephesians 5:14

Epictetus. The Complete Works of Epictetus. George Long-Comp. (2017) Independent Pub.

Galatians 6:7

Galatians 5:22

Genesis 1:27

Genesis 19:17

Isaiah 30:21

Isaiah 40:31

Isaiah 65:24

James 5:16

Jeremiah 15

Jeremiah 17:9

Jeremiah 29:11

Jeremiah 29:12-13

John 10:10

John 15:1-2

Joshua 1: 7

Joshua 1: 8

Leo Tolstoy, War and Peace, Book 15, Ch.17 Marxists Internet Archive

Luke 1:37

Luke 5:14

Luke 11:1

Luke 12:32

Luke 18:7
Mark 1
Mark 7:36
Mark 11:22
Matthew 6:33
Matthew 7:7-8
Matthew 7:24-25
Matthew 8:4
Matthew 9:29
Matthew 21:22
Philippians 4:6-7
Philippians 4:13
Philippians 4:8
Plutarch: A philosophical letter of consolation,
    (Moralia) Vol. II pp. 105
Pope John Paul II, Congregation for the
    Doctrine of the Faith, V. 24, p.8 1990
Proverbs 2:6.
Proverbs 3:5-6
Proverbs 3:21-25
Proverbs 4:6
Proverbs 4:23
Proverbs 4:27
Proverbs 13:12
Proverbs 13:20-21
Proverbs 16: 4
Psalm 20:4
Psalm 37:4
78. Psalm 37:5
Psalm 37:5-6
Psalm 145:18
Revelation 1:3

Romans 12:2
Romans 12:21
Romans 15:13
1 Thessalonians 5:17

(PART III)
Augustine, Confessions, Book X
Augustine, Sermon 277, p.15-16
Dante, (1995) Inferno: Malebolge (cantos XVIII-
    XXX). Modern Library.
Deuteronomy 4:29
Deuteronomy 8:18
Ephesians 1:11
Eclesiastés 5:18
Eclesiastés 6:10
Exodus 15:26
Exodus 20:5-6
Ezekiel 37: 1-14
Ezekiel 18:17b
Genesis 4:26
Genesis 6:3
Hosea 14:6
Isaiah 38:5
Isaiah 40: 29-31
Isaiah 40:31
James 1:17
James 4:8
Jeremiah 17:7
Jeremiah 29:13
Job 33:25
John 1:5
John 9:5

John 11:25

Jones, R. E. Socrates Bleak View of the Human Condition. 36: 97-105

Joshua 1:9

Luke 6:37

Luke 6:38

Mark 10:15

Matthew 5:2-10

Matthew 5:14-16

Matthew 9:29

Micah 6:13

Paracelsus, De Natura Rerum, Comp. by John French. Aula Lucis Press, London, UK

Philippians 4:13

Philippians 4:19

Psalm 22:3

Psalm 32:1

Proverbs 3:13

Proverbs 8:18

Proverbs 8:29

Proverbs 10:4

Proverbs 10:22

Proverbs 16:3

Proverbs 23:7

Psalm 27:1

Psalm 28:7

Psalm 37:4

Psalm 50:15

Psalm 103:5

Psalm 119:105

Ptah-hotep

Roman 12:2

Reference

Allmen, J.J. Von. (1958) A Companion to the Bible. Oxford Univ. Press.

Archer-Hid, R.D. (1935) Plato's Cosmology. Edit. Platonos Timaios. Pranava Books.

Betegh, Gabor. (2013) Pythagoreans, Orphism and Greek Religion. Univ, Cambridge.

Buret, J. Trans. (1892) The Works of Plato. O.U. Press, 3rd ed.

Bentwich, N. (1909) Philo- Judaeus of Alexadria. Jewish Pub. Society of America.

Blavatsky, H.P. (1938) The Secret Doctrine, Adyar: Theosophical Pub. House, 4th ed. Box, H. (1939) Philonis Alexandrini in Flaccum. Oxford Univ.

Campbel, A. (1969) The Book of Thoth. Samuel Weiser Inc.

Cumont, F. (1912) Astrology & Religion among the Greeks & Romans. Cosimo Classics.

Goodenough, E. R. (1935) By Light, Light; the Mystic Gospel of Hellenistic Judaism. Yale Univ. Press.

Herbert, N. (1988) Faster Than Light. New York: New American Library.

Heelan, P. A. (1965) Quantum Mechanics and Objectivity. Martinus Nijhoff Publisher.

Jeans, J. Sir. (1932) The Mysterious Universe. Kessinger Publishing.

Katz, P. (1950) Philo's Bible. Univ. Cambridge.

Moorsel, G. Van. (1955) The Mysteries of Hermes Trismegistos. Utrecht.

Oakley, Cooper I. (1942) The Comte de St. Germain. Biblioteca.

Paracelsus, De Natura Rerum, Comp.: John French. Aula Lucis Press.

Plutarch: A philosophical letter of consolation, (Moralia) Vol. II, trans. F.C. Babbitt. (1928) Loeb Classical Library.

Ryle, H. E. (1895) Philo and Holy Scripture. London & New York,

Sagan, C. (1973) The Cosmic Connection. Dell: New York.

Sarfatti, J. & Toben. B. (1975) Space-Time and Beyond. E.P. Dutton: NY, NYC

Schwartz, L (1998) Juxtaposition of Leonardo's Self-portrait and Mona Lisa.

(1911) The Oriental Religions in Roman Paganism. Chicago.

Whittaker, Sir E. (1948) Space and Spirit. Regnery: Hinsdale, Ill.